Mrs. Molesworth

Four Winds Farm And the Children of the Castle

Mrs. Molesworth

Four Winds Farm And the Children of the Castle

ISBN/EAN: 9783744713368

Printed in Europe, USA, Canada, Australia, Japan

Cover: Foto ©Thomas Meinert / pixelio.de

More available books at **www.hansebooks.com**

FOUR WINDS FARM

AND

THE CHILDREN OF THE CASTLE

FOUR WINDS FARM

AND

THE CHILDREN OF THE CASTLE

BY

MRS. MOLESWORTH

AUTHOR OF "CARROTS," "CUCKOO CLOCK," "GRANDMOTHER DEAR," ETC.

ILLUSTRATED BY WALTER CRANE

New York

MACMILLAN AND CO.

AND LONDON

1893

Norwood Press :
J. S. Cushing & Co. — Berwick & Smith.
Boston, Mass., U.S.A.

CONTENTS.

FOUR WINDS FARM.

CHAPTER VII.

CHAPTER VIII.

CHAPTER IX.

CHAPTER X.

CHAPTER XI.

CHAPTER XII.

CONTENTS.

THE CHILDREN OF THE CASTLE.

CHAPTER VII.

CHAPTER VIII.

CHAPTER IX.

CHAPTER

CHAPTER XI.

CHAPTER XII.

LIST OF ILLUSTRATIONS.

FOUR WINDS FARM.

LIST OF ILLUSTRATIONS.

THE CHILDREN OF THE CASTLE.

AND THUS SHE LED HIM OUT OF THE LARGE, COLD HALL.— page 88.
—Frontispiece.

OUR
WINDS
FARM.

BY MRS MOLESWORTH:
Author of "Carrots" "The Cuckoo Clock" &c.

ILLUSTRATED
BY
WALTER CRANE.

LONDON:
MACMILLAN & Co:
1893

First Edition 1887.   Reprinted 1891.

TO

My Youngest Daughter

OLIVE

I INSCRIBE THIS LITTLE STORY

WHICH WE THOUGHT OF

TOGETHER

London, June, 1886

" In . . . his dream he saw a child moving, and could divide the main streams, at least, of the winds that had played on him, and study so the first stage in that mental journey."

The Child in the House. — WALTER H. PATER.

FOUR WINDS FARM.

CHAPTER I.

THE VOICES IN THE CHIMNEY.

THE first thing that little Gratian Conyfer could remember in his life was hearing the wind blow. It had hushed him to sleep, it had scolded him when he was naughty, it had laughed with him at merry times, it had wailed and sobbed when he was in sorrow.

For the wind has many ways of blowing, and no one knew this better than Gratian, and no one had more right to boast an intimate acquaintance with the wind than he. You would be sure to say so yourself if you could see the place where the boy was born and bred — " Four Winds Farm."

It had not come by this name without reason, though no one still living when Gratian was a boy, could tell how long it had borne it, or by whom it had been bestowed. I wish I could take you there — were it but for five minutes, were it even in a dream. I wish I could make you *feel* what I can fancy I feel myself when I think of it — the wonderful fresh breath on one's face even on a calm day standing at the door of the farm-house, the sense of life and mischief and wild force about you, though held in check for the moment, the knowledge that the wind — the winds rather, all four of them, are there somewhere, hidden or pretending to be asleep, maybe, but ready all the same to burst out at a moment's notice. And when they do burst out — on a blowy day that is to say — ah then, I wouldn't advise you to stand at the farm-house door, unless you want to be hurled out of the way more unceremoniously than you bargained for.

It was a queer site perhaps to have chosen for a dwelling-place. Up among the moors that stretched for miles and miles on all sides, on such lofty ground that it was no wonder the trees refused to grow high, for it was hard work enough to grow at all, poor things, and to keep their footing when they had done so. They did look battered about and storm-tossed — all except the pines, who are used to that kind of life, I suppose, and did their duty manfully as sentinels on guard round the old brown house, in which, as I said, the boy Gratian first opened his baby eyes to the light.

Since that day nine winters and summers had passed. He was called a big boy now. He slept alone in a room away up a little stair by itself in a corner — an outside corner — of the farm-house. He walked, three miles there and three miles back, to school every day, carrying his books and his dinner in a satchel, along a road that would have seemed lonely and dreary to any but a moorland child—a road indeed that was little but a sheep-track the best part of the way. He spent his evenings in a corner of the large straggling kitchen, so quiet that no one would have guessed a child, above all a boy, was there; his holidays, the fine weather ones at least, out on the moor among the heather for the most part, in the company of Jonas the old shepherd, and Watch the collie dog. But he never thought his life lonely, though he had neither brother nor sister, and no one schoolfellow among the score or so at the village school that was more to him than another; he never thought about himself at all in that sort of way; he took for granted that all about him was as it should be, and if things seemed wrong sometimes he had the good sense to think it was very probably his own fault.

But he found things puzzling; he was a child who thought a great deal more than he spoke; he would not have been so puzzled if he had had more of the habit of putting his thoughts into words. Hitherto it had not seemed to matter much, life had been a simple affair, and what he did not understand he forgot about. But lately, quite lately, he had changed; his soul was beginning to grow, perhaps that was it, and felt now and then as if it wanted new clothes, and the feeling was strange. And then it isn't everybody who is born and bred where the four winds of heaven meet!

What was Gratian thinking of one Sunday evening when, quiet as usual, he sat in his corner? He had been at church and at the Sunday School; but I am afraid he could not have told you much about the sermon, and in his class he had been mildly reproved for inattention.

"You must go to bed," said his mother; "it is quite time, and you seem sleepy."

The boy rose and came round to the table at which sat his father and mother, each with a big book which Gratian knew well by sight — for it was only on Sunday evenings that the farmer and his wife had time for reading, and their books lasted them a good while. In fact they had been reading them fifty-two evenings of each year ever since the boy could recollect, and the marks, of perforated cardboard on green ribbon — his father's bore the words "Remember me," and his mother's " Forget me not " — which once, before he could read, he had regarded with mysterious awe, did not seem to him to have moved on many pages.

He stood at the table for a moment before his mother looked up; he was vaguely wondering to himself if he too would have a big book with a green ribbon-marker when he should be as old as his father and mother; did everybody? he felt half-inclined to ask his mother, but before he had decided if he should, she scattered his thoughts by glancing up at him quickly. She was quick and alert in everything she said and did, except perhaps in reading.

"Good-night, Gratian. Get quickly to bed, my boy."

"Good-night, mother, good-night, father," he said, as his mother kissed him, and his father laid his hand on the child's curly head with a kindly gesture which he only used on Sunday evenings.

"Gratian is in one of his dreams again," said the mother, when the little figure had disappeared.

" Ay," said her husband, " it's to be hoped he'll grow out of it, but he's young yet."

Gratian had stopped a moment on his way across the red-tiled passage, at one end of which was the white stone staircase; he stopped at the front door which stood slightly ajar, and stepped out into the porch. It was autumn, but early autumn only. Something of the fragrance of a summer night was still about, but there was not the calm and restfulness of the summer; on the contrary, there was a stirring and a murmuring, and the clouds overhead were scudding hurriedly before the moon, as if she were scolding them and they in a hurry to escape, thought Gratian; for there was a certain fretfulness in her air — a disquiet and unsettledness which struck him.

"Either she is angry and they are running away, or — perhaps that is it — she is sending them messages as fast as they can take them, like the rooks after they have been having a long talk together," he said to himself. Then as a figure came round the side of the house on its way to what was really the kitchen — though the big room which Gratian had just left went by the name — "Jonas," said the child aloud, "is there anything the matter up in the sky to-night?"

The old shepherd stood still; he rested the empty milkpail he was carrying on the ground, and gazed up to where Gratian was pointing.

"I cannot say," he answered, "but the summer is gone, little master. Up here the winter comes betimes, we must look for the storms and the tempests again before long."

"But not yet, oh not just yet, Jonas; I can't think why they don't get tired of fighting and rushing about and tearing each other — the winds and the rain and the clouds and all of them up there. Listen, Jonas, what is that?"

For a faint, low breath came round the end of the house like a long drawn sigh, yet with something of menace in its tone.

"Ah yes, Master Gratian. It's the winter spirit looking round a bit as I said. They'll be at it to-night, I fancy — just a spree to keep their hands in as it were. But go to bed, little master, and dream of the summer. There'll be some fine days yet awhile," and old Jonas lifted the pail again. "Madge must give this a scalding before milking time to-morrow morning, careless wench that she is," he said in a half-grumbling tone as he disappeared.

And Gratian climbed upstairs to bed.

He had a candle, and matches to light it with, in his room, but the moonlight was so bright, though fitful, that he thought it better than any candle. He undressed, not quickly as his mother had told him, I fear, standing at the curtainless window and staring out, up rather, where the clouds were still fussing about "as if they were dusting the moon's face," said Gratian to himself, laughing softly at this new fancy. And even after he was in bed he peeped out from time to time to watch the queer shadows and gleams, the quickly following light and darkness that flitted across the white walls of his little room. It was only an attic, but I think almost any little boy would have thought it a nice room. Mrs. Cony-fer kept it beautifully clean to begin with, and there was a fireplace, and a good cupboard in the wall, and a splendid view of moor and sky from the window. Gratian was very proud of his room; he had only had it a short time, only since the day he was nine years old, and it made him feel he was really grow-ing a big boy. But to-night he was hardly in his usual good spirits. It weighed on his mind that the teacher at the Sunday School had been displeased

with him; for he knew him to be kind and patient,
and Gratian liked to win his smile of approval.

"It is always the same with me," thought the
little boy, "at school every day too I am the stupidest.
I wish there were no lessons in the world. I wish
there were only birds, and lambs, and hills, and moors,
and the wind — most of all the wind, and no books
— no books, and —"

But here he fell asleep!

When he woke the room was quite dark; the
clouds had hung their dusters over the moon's face
by mistake perhaps, or else she had got tired of
shining and had turned in for a nap, thought Gratian
sleepily. He shut his eyes again, and curled himself
round the other way, and would have been asleep
again in half a minute, but for a sound which
suddenly reached his ears. Some one was talking
near him! Gratian opened his eyes again, forgetting
that that could not help him to hear, and listened.
Yes, it was a voice — two voices; he heard one stop
and the other reply, and now and then they seemed
to be talking together, and gradually as he listened
he discovered that they came from the direction of
the fireplace. Could it be the voices of his father
and mother coming up from below, through the
chimney, somehow? No, their voices were not so
strangely soft and sadly sweet; besides their room
was not under his, nor did they ever talk in the
middle of the night.

" They are too sleepy for that," thought Gratian with a little smile. For the farmer and his wife were very hard-working, and even on Sunday they were tired. It was a long walk to church, and unless the weather were very bad they always went twice.

Gratian listened again, more intently than ever. The voices went on : he could distinguish the different tones — more than two he began to fancy. But how provoking it was : he *could* not catch the words. And from the strain of listening he almost began to fall asleep again, when at last — yes, there was no doubt of it now — he caught the sound of his own name.

" Gratian, Gra—tian," in a very soft inquiring tone ; " ye—es, he is a good boy on the whole, but he is foolish too. He is wasting his time."

" Sadly so — sad—ly so—o," hummed back the second voice. " He only dreams — dreams are very well in their way, they are a beginning sometimes, so—me—ti—imes. But he will never do any-thing even with his dreams unless he works too—wo—orks too."

" Ah no — no—o. All must work save the will-o'-the-wisps, and what good are they ? What good are the—ey ? "

Then the two, or the three, maybe even the four, Gratian could not be sure but that there were perhaps four, voices seemed all to hum together, " What good are the—cy?" Till with a sudden rushing call one broke in with a new cry.

"Sisters," it said, "we must be off. Our work awai—aits us, awai—aits us."

And softly they all faded away, or was it perhaps that Gratian fell asleep?

He woke the next morning with a confused remembrance of what he had heard, and for some little time he could not distinguish how much he had dreamt from what had reached his ears before he fell asleep. For all through the night a vague feeling had haunted him of the soft, humming murmur, and two or three times when he half woke and turned on his side, he seemed to hear again the last echoes of the voices in the chimney.

"But it couldn't have been them." he said to himself as he sat up in his little bed, his hands clasped round his knees, as he was very fond of sitting: "They said they were going away to their work. What work could they have — voices, just voices in the chimney? And they said I was wasting my time. What did they mean? *I'm* not like a will-o'-the-wisp; I don't dance about and lead people into bogs. I — "

But just then his mother's voice sounded up the stairs.

"Gratian — aren't you up yet? Father is out, and the breakfast will be ready in ten minutes. Quick, quick, my boy."

Gratian started; he put one pink foot out of bed and looked at it as if he had never seen five toes before, then he put out the other, and at last found himself altogether on the floor. It was rather a chilly morning, and he was only allowed cold water in a queer old tub that he could remember being dreadfully afraid of when he was a *very* little boy — it had seemed so big to him then. But he was not so babyish now; he plunged bravely into the old tub, and the shock of the cold completely awakened him, so that he looked quite bright and rosy when he came into the kitchen a few minutes later.

His mother looked up from the pot of oatmeal porridge she was ladling out into little bowls for the breakfast.

"That's right," she said; "you look better than you did last night. Try and have a good day at school to-day, Gratian. Monday's always the best day for a fresh start."

Gratian listened, but did not answer. It generally took him a good while to get his speeches ready, except perhaps when he was alone with Jonas and Watch. It seemed easier to him to speak to Jonas than to anybody else. He began eating his porridge — slowly, porridge and milk spoonfuls turn about, staring before him as he did so.

"Mother," he said at last, " is it naughty to dream?"

"Naughty to dream," repeated his mother, "what do you mean? To dream when you're asleep?"

"No — I don't think it's that kind," began the child, but his mother interrupted him. Her own words of the night before returned to her mind. Could Gratian have overheard them?

"You mean dreaming when you should be working, perhaps?" she said. "Well, yes — without saying it's naughty, it's certainly not good. It's wasting one's time. Everybody's got work to do in this world, and it needs all one's attention. You'll find it out for yourself, but it's a good thing to find it out young. Most things are harder to learn old than young, Gratian."

Gratian listened, but again without speaking.

"It's very queer," he was thinking to himself — "mother says the same thing."

CHAPTER II.

AT SCHOOL.

C. C. Fraser Tytler.

GRATIAN shouldered his satchel and set off to school. He had some new thoughts in his head this morning, but still he was not too busy with them to forget to look about him. It was evident that old Jonas had been right; the storm spirits had been about in the night. The fallen autumn leaves which had been lying in heaps the day before were scattered everywhere, the little pools of water left by yesterday's rain had almost disappeared, overhead the clouds were gradually settling down in quiet masses as if tired and sleepy with the rushing about of the night before.

It was always fresh up at Four Winds Farm, but to-day there was a particularly brisk and inspiriting feeling in the air; and as Gratian ran down the bit of steep hill between the gate and the road which he partially followed to school, he laughed to himself as a little wind came kissing him on the cheek.

" Good-morning, wind," he said aloud. " Which

of them are you, I wonder?"   And some old verses
he had often heard his mother say came into his
head —

"North winds send hail,
　　South winds bring rain,
　East winds we bewail,
　　West winds blow amain."

"I think you must be west wind, but you're not
blowing amain this morning. Never mind; you can
when you like, I know. *You* can work with a will.
There now — how funny — I'm saying it myself;
I wonder if that's what the voices meant I should
do — work with a will, work with a will," and
Gratian sang the words over softly to himself as he
ran along.

As I said, his road to school was a great part of
the way nothing but a sheep-track. It was not that
there did not exist a proper road, but this proper
road, naturally enough, went winding about a good
deal, for it was meant for carts and horses as well as
or more than for little boys, and no carts or horses
could ever have got along it had the road run in a
direct line from the Farm to the village. For the
village lay low and the Farm very high. Gratian
followed the road for the first half-mile or so, that is
to say as long as he could have gained nothing by
quitting it, but then came a corner at which he left
it to meander gradually down the high ground, while
he scrambled over a low wall of loose stones and

found himself on what he always considered his own particular path. At this point began the enjoyment of his walk, for a few minutes carried him round the brow of the hill, out of sight of the road and of everything save the sky above and the great stretching moorland beneath. And this was what Gratian loved. He used to throw himself on the short tufty grass, his elbows on the ground, and his chin in his hands — his satchel wherever it liked, and lie there gazing and dreaming and wishing he could stay thus always.

He did the same thing this morning, but somehow his dreams were not quite so undisturbed. He was no longer sure that he would like to lie there always doing nothing but dreaming, and now that he had got this idea into his head everything about him seemed to be repeating it. He looked at the heather, faded and dull now, and remembered how, a while ago, the bees had been hard at work on the moors gathering their stores. "What a lot of trouble it must be to make honey!" he thought. He felt his own little rough coat, and smiled to think that not so very long ago it had been walking about the hills on a different back. "It isn't much trouble for the sheep to let their wool grow, certainly," he said to himself, "but it's a lot of work for lots of people before wool is turned into a coat for a little boy. Nothing can be done without work, I suppose, and I'd rather be a bee than a sheep a good deal, though

I'd rather be old Watch than either, and *he* works hard — yes, he certainly does."

And then suddenly he remembered that if he didn't bestir himself he would be late at school, which wouldn't be at all the good start his mother had advised him to make as it was Monday morning.

He went on pretty steadily for the rest of the way, only stopping about six times, and that not for long together, otherwise he certainly would not have got to school before morning lessons were over. But, as it was, he got an approving nod from the teacher for being in very good time. For the teacher could not help liking Gratian, though, as a pupil, he gave him plenty of trouble, seeming really sometimes as if he *could* not learn.

"And yet," thought the master — for he was a young man who did think — "one cannot look into the child's face without seeing there are brains behind it, and brains of no common kind maybe. But I haven't got the knack of making him use them; for nine years old he is exceedingly stupid."

Things went bettter to-day. Gratian was full of his new ideas and really meant to try. But even trying with all one's might and main won't build Rome in a day. Gratian had idled and dreamed through lesson-time too often to lose the bad habit all at once. He saw himself passed as usual by children younger than he, who had been a much shorter time at school, and his face grew very melancholy, and two or three big tears gathered more than once in his eyes while he began to say in his own mind that trying was no good.

Morning school was over at twelve; most of the children lived in the village, and some but a short way off, so that they could easily run home for their dinner and be back in time for afternoon lessons; Gratian Conyfer was the only one whose home was too far off for him to go back in the middle of the day. So he brought his dinner with him and ate it in winter beside the schoolroom fire, in summer in a corner of the playground, where, under a tree, stood an old bench. This was the dining-room he liked best, and though now summer was past and autumn indeed fast fading into winter, Gratian had not yet deserted his summer quarters, and here the school-master found him half an hour or so before it was time for the children's return.

"Are you not cold there, my boy?" he asked kindly.

"No, thank you, sir," Gratian answered, and looking more closely at him the master saw he had been crying.

"What is the matter, Gratian?" he asked. "You've not been quarrelling or fighting I'm sure, you never do, and as for lessons they went a bit better to-day, I think, didn't they?"

But at these words Gratian only turned his face to the wall and wept — wiping his eyes from time to time on the cuff of the linen blouse which he wore at school over his coat.

The schoolmaster's heart was touched, though he was pretty well used to tears. But Gratian's seemed different somehow.

"What is it, my boy?" he said again.

"It's — it's just that, sir — lessons, I mean. I did try, sir. I meant to work with a will, I did indeed."

"But you did do better. I knew you were trying," said the teacher quietly.

Gratian lifted his tear-stained face and looked at the master in surprise.

"Did you, sir?" he said. "It seemed to me to go worser and worser."

"No, I didn't think so. And sometimes, Gratian, when we think we are doing worse, it shows we are really doing better. We're getting up a little higher, you see, and beginning to look on and to see how far we have to go, and that we might have got on faster. When we're not climbing at all, but just staying lazily at the foot of the hill, we don't know anything about how steep and high it is."

Gratian had quite left off crying by now and was listening attentively. The master's words needed no explanation to him; he had caught the sense and meaning at once.

"Everybody has to work if they're to do any good, haven't they, sir?" he asked.

"*Everybody*," agreed the master.

" But wouldn't it be better if everybody *liked* their work — couldn't they do it better if they did?" he asked. " That's what I'm vexed about, partly. I don't *like* lessons, sir," he said in a tone of deep conviction. " I'm afraid I'm too stupid ever to like them."

The schoolmaster could scarcely keep from smiling.

" You're not so very old yet, Gratian," he said. " It's just possible you may change. Besides, in some ways the beginning's the worst. You can't read very easily yet — not well enough to enjoy reading to yourself?"

" No, sir," said the boy, hanging his head again.

" Well, then, wait a while and see if you don't change about books and lessons."

" And if I don't ever change," said Gratian earnestly. " Can people ever do things well that they don't like doing?"

The schoolmaster looked at him. It was a curious question for a boy of nine years old.

" Yes," he said, " I hope so, indeed," and his mind went back to a time when he had looked forward to being something very different from a village schoolmaster, when he could have fancied no employment could be less to his liking than teaching. " I hope so, indeed," he repeated. " And if you work with a will you — get to like the work whatever it is."

" Thank you, sir," said the boy, and the master turned away. Then a thought struck him.

"What do you best like doing, Gratian?"

The boy hesitated. Then he grew a little red.

"It isn't doing anything really," he said; "it's what mother calls dreaming — out on the moors, sir, that's the best of all — with the wind all about, and nothing but it and the moor and the sky. And the feel of it keeps in me. Even when I'm at home in the kitchen by the fire, if I shut my eyes I can fancy it."

The master nodded his head.

"Dreaming is no harm in its right place. But if one did nothing but dream, the dreams would lose their colour, I expect."

"That's something like what *they* said, again," thought the boy to himself.

The schoolmaster walked away. "A child with something uncommon about him, I fancy," he said in his mind. "One sees that sometimes in a child living as much alone with nature as he does. But I scarcely think he's clever, and then the rough daily life will most likely nip in the bud any sort of poetry or imagination that there may be germs of."

He didn't quite understand Gratian, and then, too, he didn't take into account what it is to be born under the protection of the four winds of heaven.

But Gratian felt much happier after his talk with the master, and afternoon lessons went better. They were generally easier than the morning ones, and often more interesting. This afternoon it was a geography lesson. The master drew out the great frame with the big maps hanging on it, and explained to the children as he went along. It was about the north to-day, far away up in the north, where the ice-fields spread for hundreds of miles and everything is in a sleep of whiteness and silence. And Gratian listened with parted lips and earnest eyes. He seemed to see it all. "I wish I knew as much as he does," he thought. "I wish I could read it in books to myself."

And for the first time there came home to him a faint, shadowy feeling of what books are — of the treasures buried in the rows and rows of little black letters that he so often wished had never been invented.

"Yes," he said to himself, "I'll try to learn so that I can read it all to myself."

It was growing already a little dusk when he set off on his walk home. The evenings were beginning "to draw in" as the country folk say.

But little cared the merry throng who poured out of the schoolroom gate as five o'clock rang from the church clock, clattering, racing, tumbling over each other, pushing, pulling, shouting, but all in play. For they are a good-natured set, though rough and ready — these hardy moor children. And they grow into honest and sturdy men and women, hospitable and kindly, active and thrifty, though they care for little beyond their own corner of the world, and would scarcely find it out if all the books and "learn-ing" in existence were suddenly made an end of.

There are mischievous imps among them, neverthe-less, and none was more so than Tony, the miller's son. He meant no harm, but he loved teasing, and Gratian, gentle and silent, was often a tempting victim. This evening, as sometimes happened, a dozen or so of the children whose homes lay at the end of the village, past which was the road to the Farm, went on together.

"We'll run a bit of the road home with thee, Gratian," said Tony.

And though the boy did not much care for their company, he thought it would be unfriendly to say so, nor did he like to refuse when Tony insisted on carrying his satchel for him. "There's no books in mine," he said; "I took them home at dinner-time, and I'm sure your shoulders will be aching before you get to the Farm with the weight of yours. My goodness, how many books have you got in it? I say," as he pretended to examine them, "here's Gratian Conyfer going to be head o' the school, and put us all to shame with his learning."

But as Gratian said nothing he seemed satisfied, and after stopping a minute or two to arrange the satchel again, ran after the others.

"It's getting dark, Tony," said his sister Dolly, "we mustn't go farther. Good-night, Gratian, we've brought you a bit of your way — Tony, and

Ralph, and I," for the other children had gradually fallen off.

"Yes—a good mile of it, thank you, Dolly. And thank you, Tony, for helping me with my satchel—that's right, thank you," as Tony was officiously fastening it on.

"Good-night," said Tony: "you're no coward anyway, Gratian. I shouldn't like to have all that way to go in the dark, for it will be dark soon. There are queer things to be seen on the moor after sunset, folks say."

"Ay, so they say," said Ralph.

"I'll be home in no time," Gratian called back. For he did not know what fear was.

But after he had ran awhile, he felt more tired than usual. Was it perhaps the fit of crying he had had at dinner-time that made him so weary? He plodded on, however, shifting his satchel from time to time, it felt so strangely heavy, and queer tales he had heard of the little mountain man that would jump on your shoulders, and cling on till he had strangled you, unless you remembered the right spell to force him off with; or of the brownies who catch children with invisible ropes, and make them run round and round without their knowing they have left the straight road till they drop with fatigue, came into his mind.

"There must be something wrong with my satchel," he said at last, and he pulled it round so that he could open it. He drew his hand out with a cry of vexation and distress. Tony, yes it must have been Tony — though at first he was half-inclined to think the mountain men or the brownies had been playing their tricks on him — Tony had filled the satchel with heavy stones, and had no doubt taken out the books at the time he was pretending to examine them. It was too bad. And what had he done with the books?

"He may have taken them home with him, he may have hidden them and get them as he passses by, or he may have left them on the moor, and if it rains they'll be spoilt, and the copy-books are sure to blow away."

For in his new ardour, Gratian had brought home books of all kinds, meaning to work so well that his master should be quite astonished the next day, and the poor little fellow sat down on the heather, his arms and shoulders aching and sore, and let the tears roll down his face.

Suddenly a slight sound, something between a murmur and a rustle, some little way from him, made him look round. It was an unusually still evening; Gratian had scarcely ever known the moorland road so still — it could not be the wind then! He looked round him curiously, and for a moment or two forgot his troubles in his wonder as to what it could be. There it was again, and the boy started to his feet.

CHAPTER III.

FLYING VISITS.

Yes — he heard it again, and this time it sounded almost like voices speaking. He turned to the side whence it came, and to his surprise, in the all but darkness, there glimmered for an instant or two a sudden light. It was scarcely indeed to be called light; it was more like the reflection of faint colour on the dark background.

"It is like a black rainbow," said Gratian to himself. "I wonder if there are some sorts of rainbows that come in the night. I wonder —" but suddenly a waft of soft though fresh air on his cheek made him start. All around him, but an instant before, had been so still that he could not understand it, and his surprise was not lessened when a voice sounded close to his ear.

"What about your books, Gratian? How are you going to find them?"

The boy turned to look who was speaking. His first thought was that one of his companions, knowing of the trick Tony had played him, had run after him with the books. But the figure beside him was not that of one of his companions — was it that of any one at all? Gratian rubbed his eyes: the faint light that remained, — the last rays of reflected sunset — were more bewildering than decided night; was it fancy that he had heard a voice speaking? was it fancy that he had seen a waving, fluttering form beside him?

No, there it was again; softly moving garments, with something of a green radiance on them, a sweet, fair face, like a face in a dream, seen but for an instant and then hidden again by a wave of mist that seemed to come between it and him, a gentle yet cheery voice repeating again —

"What of the books, Gratian? How are you going to find them?"

"I don't know," said the boy. "Who are you? How do you know about them, and can you help me to find them?"

But the sound of his own voice, rough and sharp, and yet thick it somehow seemed, in comparison with the soft clearness of the tones he had just heard, fell on his ears strangely. It seemed to awake him.

"Am I dreaming?" he said to himself. "There is no one there. How silly of me to speak to nobody! I might as well be speaking to the wind!"

"Exactly," said the voice, followed this time by

WAS IT FANCY THAT HE HAD SEEN A WAVING, FLUTTERING FORM BESIDE HIM ? — p. 26.

a little burst of the sweetest laughter Gratian had ever heard. "Come, Gratian, don't be so dull: what's wrong with your eyes? Come, dear, if you do want to find your books, that's to say. You see me now, don't you?"

And again the fresh waft passed across his cheeks, and again the flutter of radiant green and the fair face caught his eyes.

"Yes," he said, "I see you now — or — or I did see you half a second ago," for even while he said it the vision had seemed to fade.

"That's right — then come."

He was opening his lips to ask how and where, but he had not time, nor did he need to do so. The breeze, slight as it was, seemed to draw him onwards, and the faint, quivering green light gleamed out from moment to moment before him. It was evident which way he was to go. Only for an instant a misgiving came over him and he hesitated.

"I say," he called out, "you mustn't be offended, but you're not a will-o'-the-wisp, are you? I don't want to follow one of them. They're no good."

Again the soft laughter, but it sounded kind and pleasant, not the least mocking.

"That's right. Never have anything to say to will-o'-the-wisps, Gratian. But I'm not one — see — I keep on my way. I don't dance and jerk from side to side."

It was true; it was wonderful how fast she — if it

were she, the voice sounded like a woman's — got
over the ground and Gratian after her, without
faltering or stumbling or even getting out of breath.

"Here we are," she said, "stoop down. Gratian —
there are your books hidden beside the furze bush
at your feet. And it is going to rain; they would
have been quite spoilt by morning even if I had done
my best. It was an ugly trick of Master Tony's.
There now, have you got them?"

"Yes, thank you," said Gratian, fumbling for his
satchel, still hanging round his shoulders, though to
his surprise empty, for he did not remember having
thrown the stones out, "I have got them all now.
Thank you *very* much whoever you are. I would
like to kiss you if only I could see you long enough
at a time."

But a breath like a butterfly's kiss fluttered on to
his cheek, and the gleam of two soft bluey-green eyes
seemed for the hundredth part of a second to dance
into his own.

"I have kissed you," said the voice, now sounding
farther away, "and not for the first nor the thou-
sandth time, if you had known it! But you are
waking up a little now; our baby boy is learning to
see and to hear and to feel. Good-bye — good-night,
Gratian. Work your best with your books to-night
— get home as fast as you can. By the bye it is
late; shall I speed you on your way? You will
know how far that is to-morrow morning — look for

the furze bush on the right of the path when it turns for the last time, and you will see if I don't know how to help you home in no time."

And almost before the last words had faded, Gratian felt himself gently lifted off his feet — a rush, a soft whiz, and he was standing by the Farm gate, while before him shone out the warm ruddy glow from the unshuttered windows of the big kitchen, and his mother's voice, as she heard the latch click, called out to him —

"Is that you, Gratian? You are very late; if it had not been such a very still, beautiful evening I should really have begun to think you had been blown away coming over the moor."

And Gratian rubbed his eyes as he came blinking into the kitchen. His mother's words puzzled him, though he knew she was only joking. It *was* a very still night — that was the funny part of it.

"Why, you look for all the world as if you'd been having a nap, my boy," she went on, and Gratian stood rubbing his hands before the fire, wondering if perhaps he had. He was half-inclined to tell his mother of Tony's trick and what had come of it. But she might say he had dreamt it, and then it would seem ill-natured to Tony.

"And I don't want mother and father to think I'm always dreaming and fancying," he thought to himself, for just at that moment the farmer's footsteps were heard as he came in to supper. "Anyway I want them to see I mean to get on better at school than I have done."

He did not speak much at table, but he tried to help his mother by passing to her whatever she wanted, and jumping up to fetch anything missing. And it was a great pleasure when his father once or twice nodded and smiled at him approvingly.

"He's getting to be quite a handy lad—eh, mother?" he said.

As soon as supper was over and cleared away, Gratian set to work at his lessons with a light heart. It was wonderful how much easier and more interesting they seemed now that he really gave his whole attention, and especially since he had tried to understand what the teacher had said about them.

"If only I had tried like this before, how much further on I should be now," he could not help saying to himself with a sigh. "And the queer thing is, that the more I try the more I want to try. My head begins to feel so much tidier."

But with all the good-will in the world, at nine years old a head cannot do *very* much at a time. Gratian had finished all the lessons he *had* to do for the next day and was going back in his books with the wish to learn over again, and more thoroughly, much that he had not before really taken in or understood, when to his distress his poor little head bumped down on to the volume before him, and he found by the start that he was going to sleep! Still it wasn't very late — mother had said nothing yet about bedtime.

"It is that I have got into such a stupid, lazy way of learning, I suppose," he said to himself, getting up from his seat. "Perhaps the air will wake me up a bit," and he went through the little entrance hall and stood in the porch, looking out.

It was a very different night from the last. All was so still and calm that for once the name of the Farm did not seem to suit it.

Gratian leant against the door-post, looking up to the sky, and just then, like the evening before, old Jonas, followed by Watch, came round the corner.

"Good-evening, Jonas," said the boy. "How quiet it is to-night! There wasn't much of a storm after all."

"No, Master Gratian," replied the shepherd; "I told you they were only a-knocking about a bit to keep their hands in;" and he too stood still and looked up at the sky.

"I don't like it so still as this," said the boy. "It doesn't seem right. I came out here for a breath of air to wake me up. I've been working hard at my lessons, Jonas; I'm going always to work hard now. But I wish I wasn't sleepy."

"Sign that you've worked enough for to-night, maybe," said Jonas. But as he spoke, Gratian started.

"Jonas," he said, "did you see a sort of light

down there — across the grass there in front, a sort of golden-looking flash? ah, there it is again," and just at the same moment a soft, almost warm waft of air seemed to float across his face, and Gratian fancied he heard the words, " good boy, good boy."

" 'Tis a breath of south wind getting up," said old Jonas quietly. " I've often thought to myself that there's colours in the winds, Master Gratian, though folk would laugh at me for an old silly if I said so."

"*Colours*," repeated Gratian, " do you mean many colours? I wasn't saying anything about the wind though, Jonas — did you feel it too? It was over there — look, Jonas — it seemed to come from behind the big bush."

" Due south, due south," said Jonas. " And golden yellow is my fancy for the south."

" And what for the north, and for the — " began Gratian eagerly, but his mother's voice interrupted him.

" Bedtime, Gratian," she called, " come and put away your books. You've done enough lessons for to-night."

Gratian gave himself a little shake of impatience.

" How tiresome," he said. " I am quite awake now. I want you to go on telling me about the winds, Jonas, and I want to do a lot more lessons. I can't go to bed yet," but even while the words were on his lips, he started and shivered. " Jonas, it can't be south wind. It's as cold as anything."

For a sharp keen gust had suddenly come round the corner, rasping the child's unprotected face almost "like a knife" as people sometimes say, and Watch, who had been rubbing his nose against Gratian, gave a snort of disgust.

"You see Watch feels it too," said the boy. But Jonas only turned a little and looked about him calmly.

"I can't say as I felt it, Master Gratian," he said. "But there's no answering for the winds and their freaks here at the Four Winds Farm, and it's but natural you should know more about 'em than most. All the same, I take it as you're feeling cold and chilly-like means as bed is the best place. You're getting sleepy — to say nothing of the Missus calling to ye to go."

And again the mother's voice was heard.

"Gratian, Gratian, my boy. Don't you hear me?"

He moved, but slowly. A little imp of opposition had taken up its abode in the boy. Perhaps he had been feeling too pleased with his own good resolutions and beginnings!

"Too bad," he muttered to himself, "just when I was getting to understand my lessons better. Old Jonas is very stupid."

Again the short, sharp cutting slap of cold air on his face, and in spite of himself the boy moved more quickly.

"Good-night, Jonas," he said rather grumpily,

though he would not let himself shiver for fear he should again be told it showed he was sleepy, " I'm going. I'm not at all tired, but I'm going all the same. Only how can you say it's south wind — ! "

" I don't say so now. I said it *was* south — that soft feeling as if one could see the glow of the south in it. Like enough it's east by now ; isn't this where all the winds meet ? Well, I'm off too. Good-night, master."

" And you'll tell me about all the colours another time, won't you, Jonas ? " said Gratian in a mollified tone.

" Or you'll tell me, maybe," said the old man. " Never fear — we'll have some good talks over it. Out on the moor some holiday, with nobody but the sheep and Watch to hear our fancies — that's the best time — isn't it ? "

And the old shepherd whistled to the dog and disappeared round the corner of the house.

His mother met Gratian at the kitchen door.

" I was coming out to look for you," she said. " Put away your books now. You'd do no more good at them to-night."

" I wasn't sleepy, mother. I went to the door to wake myself up," he replied. But his tone was no longer fretful or cross.

" Feeling you needed waking up was something very like being sleepy," she answered smiling. " And all the lessons you have to learn are not to be found in your books, Gratian."

He did not at once understand, but he kept the words in his mind to think over.

"Good-night, mother," and he lifted his soft round face for her kiss.

"Good-night, my boy. Father has gone out to the stable to speak to one of the men. I'll say good-night to him for you. Pleasant dreams, and get up as early as you like if you want to work more."

"Mother," said Gratian hesitatingly.

"Well?"

"Is it a good thing to be born where the four winds meet?"

She laughed.

"I can't say," she replied. "It's not done you any harm so far. But don't begin getting your head full of fancies, my boy. Off with you to bed, and get to sleep as fast as you can. Pleasant dreams."

"But, mother," said the child as he went upstairs, "dreams are fancies."

"Yes, but they don't waste our time. There's no harm in dreaming when we're asleep — we can't be doing aught else then."

"Oh," said Gratian, "it's dreaming in the day that wastes time then."

He was turning the corner of the stair as he said so, speaking more to himself than to his mother. Just then a little waft of air came right in his face. It was not the sharp touch that had made him start at the door, nor was it the soft warm breath which old Jonas said was the south wind. Rather did it remind Gratian of the kindly breeze and the sea-green glimmerings on the moor. He stood still for an instant. Again it fluttered by him, and he heard the words, " Not always, Gratian ; not always."

" What was I saying ? " he asked himself. " Ah yes — that it is dreaming in the day that is a waste of time ! And now she says ' Not always.' You are very puzzling people whoever you are," he went on ; " you whose voices I hear in the chimney, and who seem to know all I am thinking whether I say it or not."

And as he lifted his little face towards the corner whence the sudden draught had come, there fell on his ears the sound of rippling laughter — the merriest and yet softest laughter he had ever heard, and in which several voices seemed to mingle. So near it seemed at first that he could have fancied it came from the old granary on the other side of the wooden partition shutting off the staircase, but again, in an instant, it seemed to dance and flicker itself away, till nothing remained but a faint ringing echo, which might well be no more than the slight rattle of the glass in the old casement window.

Then all was silent, and the boy went on to his own room, and was soon covered up and fast asleep in his little white bed.

There were no voices in the chimney that night, or if there were Gratian did not hear them. But he had a curious dream.

CHAPTER IV.

A RAINBOW DANCE.

"Purple and azure, white and green and golden,
*   *   *   *   *
and they whirl
Over each other with a thousand motions."

Prometheus Unbound. — SHELLEY.

HE dreamt that he awoke, and found himself not in his comfortable bed in his own room, but in an equally comfortable but much more uncommon bed in a very different place. Out on the moor! He opened his eyes and stared about him in surprise; there were the stars, up overhead, all blinking and winking at him as if asking what business a little boy had out there among them all in the middle of the night. And when he did find out where he was, he felt still more surprised at being so warm and cosy. For he felt perfectly so, even though he had neither blankets nor sheets nor pillow, but instead of all these a complete nest of the softest moss all about him. He was lying on it, and it covered him over as perfectly as a bird is covered by its feathers.

"Dear me," he said to himself, "this is very funny. How have I got here, and who has covered me up like this?"

But still he did not feel so excessively surprised as if he had been awake; for in dreams, as everybody knows, any surprise one feels quickly disappears, and one is generally very ready to take things as they come. So he lay still, just quietly gazing about him. And gradually a murmur of approaching sound caught his ears. It was like soft voices and fluttering garments and breezes among trees, all mixed together, till as it came nearer the voices detached themselves from the other sounds, and he heard what they were saying.

" Yes, he deserves a treat, poor child," said one in very gentle caressing tones; "you have teased him enough, sisters."

"Teased him!" exclaimed another voice, and this time it seemed a familiar one to him; "*I* tease him! Why, as you well know, it is my mission in life to comfort and console. I don't believe in petting and praising to the same extent as you do, perhaps — still you cannot say I ever tease. Laugh at him a little now and then, I may. But that does no harm."

" I never pet and praise except when it is deserved," murmured the first voice — and as he heard its soft tones a sort of delicious languor seemed to creep over Gratian — "never. But I beg your pardon, sister, if I misjudged you. You can be rigorous sometimes, you know, and — "

"So much the better — so much the better," broke in with clear cutting distinctness another voice;

"how would the world go round — that is to say, how would the ships sail and the windmills turn — if we were all four as sweet and silky as you, my golden-winged sister? But it was *I* who teased the child as you call it — I slapped him on the face; yes, and I am ready to do it again — to sting him sharply, when I think he needs it."

"Right, right — quite right," said another voice, not exactly sharp and clear like the last, yet with a resemblance to it, though deeper and sterner and with a strange cold strength in its accents. "You are his true friend in doing so. I for my part shall always be ready to invigorate and support him — to brace him for the battles he must fight. But you, sister, have a rare gift of correction and of discerning the weak points which may lead to defeat and failure. Yours is an ungrateful task truly, but you are a valuable monitor."

"I must find my satisfaction in such considerations; it is plain I shall never get any elsewhere," replied the former speaker, rather bitterly. "What horrid things are said of me, to be sure! Every ache and pain is laid at my door — I am 'neither good for man nor beast,' I am told! and yet — I am not all grim and gray, am I, sisters? There is a rosy glow in the trail of my garments if people were not so short-sighted and colour-blind."

"True, indeed, as who knows better than I," said the sweet mellow tones of the first speaker. "When you come my way and we dance together, sister, who could be less grim than you?"

" Ah, indeed," said the cold, stern voice, but it sounded less stern now, "then her sharp and biting words came from neighbourhood with *me*. Ah well —I can bear the reproach."

" I should think so," said the voice which Gratian had recognised, "for you know in your heart, you great icy creature, that you love fun as well as any one. How you do whirl and leap and rush and tear about, once your spirits really get the better of you! And you have such pretty playthings — your snow-flakes and filigree and icicles — none of us can boast such treasures, not to speak of your icebergs and crystal palaces, where you hide heaven knows what. My poor waves and foam, though I allow they are pretty in their way, are nothing to your possessions."

" Never mind all that. *I* don't grumble, though I might. What can one do with millions of tons of sand for a toy, I should like to know? And little else comes in my way that I can play catch-and-toss with! I can waft my scents about, to be sure — there is some pleasure in that. But now for our dance — our rainbow dance, sisters — no need to wake him roughly. We need only kiss his eyelids."

And Gratian, who had not all this time, strange to say, known that his eyes were closed again, felt across his lids a breeze so fresh and sudden that he naturally unclosed them to see whence it came. And

"NOW FOR OUR DANCE—OUR RAINBOW DANCE, SISTERS—NO NEED TO
WAKE HIM ROUGHLY. WE NEED ONLY KISS HIS EYELIDS."—p. 40.

once open he did not feel inclined to shut them again, I can assure you.

The sight before him was so pretty — and not the sight only. For the voices had melted into music — far off at first, then by slow degrees coming nearer; rising, falling, swelling, sinking, bright with rejoicing like the song of the lark, then soft and low as the tones of a mother hushing her baby to sleep, again wildly triumphant like a battle strain of victory, and even while you listened changing into the mournful, solemn cadence of a dirge, till at last all mingled into a slow, even measure of stately harmony, and the colours which had been weaving themselves in the distance, like a plaited rainbow before the boy's eyes, took definite form as they drew near him.

He saw them then — the four invisible sisters; he saw them, and yet it is hard to tell what he saw! They were distinct and yet vague, separate and yet together. But by degrees he distinguished them better. There was his old friend with the floating sea-green-and-blue mantle, and the streaming fair hair and loving sad eyes, and next her the sister with the golden wings and glowing locks and laughing rosy face, and then a gray shrouded nimble figure, which seemed everywhere at once, whose features Gratian could scarcely see, though a pair of bright sparkling eyes flashed out now and then, while sometimes a gleam of radiant red lighted up the grim robe. And in and out in the meshes of the dance glided the white form of the genius of the north — cold and stately, sparkling as she moved, though shaded now and then by the steel-blue veil which covered the dusky head. But as the dance went on, the music gradually grew faster and the soft regular movements changed into a quicker measure. In and out the four figures wove and unwove themselves together, and the more quickly they moved the more varied and brilliant grew the colours which seemed a part of them, so that each seemed to have all those of the others as well as her own, and Gratian understood why they had spoken of the rainbow dance. Golden-wings glowed with every other shade reflected on her own rich background, the sister from the sea grew warmer with the red and yellow that shone out among the lapping folds of her mantle, with its feather-like trimming of foam, the gray of the East-wind's garments grew ruddier, like the sky before sunrise, and the cold white of the icy North glimmered and gleamed like an opal. And faster and faster they danced and glided and whirled about, till Gratian felt as if his breath were going, and that in another moment he would be carried away himself by the rush.

"Stop, stop," he cried at last. "It is beautiful, it is lovely, but my breath is going. Stop."

Instantly the four heads turned towards him, the four pairs of wings sheathed themselves, the eyes, laughing and gentle, piercing and grave, seemed all to be gazing at him at once, and eight outstretched arms seemed as if about to lift him upwards.

"No — no — " he said, "I don't want — I don't — "

But with the struggle to speak he awoke. He was in his own bed of course, and by the light he saw that it must be nearly time to get up.

He stretched himself sleepily, smiling as he did so.

"What nice dreams I have had," he said to himself. "I wonder if they come of working well at my lessons? *They* said it was to be a treat for me. I wish I could go to sleep and dream it all over again."

But just then he heard his mother's voice calling up the stair to him.

"Are you up, Gratian? You will be late if you are not quick."

Gratian gave himself a little shake of impatience under the bedclothes; he glanced at the window — the sky was gray and overcast, with every sign of a rainy day about it. He tucked himself up again, even though he knew it was very foolish thus to delay the evil moment.

"It's too bad," he thought. "I can *never* do what I want. Last night I had to go to bed when I wanted to sit up, and now I have to get up when I do so want to stay in bed."

But just at that moment a strange thing happened. The little casement window burst open with a bang, and a blast of cold sharp wind dashed into the room, upsetting a chair, scattering Gratian's clothes, neatly laid together in a little heap, and flinging itself on the bed with a whirl, so that the coverlet took to playing antics in its turn, and the blankets no doubt would have followed its example had Gratian not clutched at them. But all his comfort was destroyed — no possibility of feeling warm and snug with the window open and all this uproar going on. Gratian sprang up in a rage, and ran to the window. He shut it again easily enough.

"I can't think what made it fly open," he said to himself; "there was no wind in the night, and it never burst open before."

He stood shivering and undecided. Now that the window was shut, bed looked very comfortable again.

"I'll just get in for five minutes," he said to himself; "I'm so shivering cold with that wind, I shan't get warm all day."

He turned to the bed, but just as one little foot was raised to get in, lo and behold, a rattle and bang, and again the window burst open! Gratian flew back, it shut obediently as before. But he was now thoroughly awakened and alert. There was no good going back to bed if he was to be blown out of it in this fashion, and Gratian set to to dress himself, though in a rather surly mood, and keeping an eye on the rebellious window the while. But the window behaved quite well — it showed no signs of bursting open, it did not even rattle! and Gratian was ready in good time after all.

"You look cold, my boy," said his mother, when he was seated at table and eating his breakfast.

"The wind blew my window open twice, and it made my room very cold," he replied rather dolefully.

"Blew your window open? That's strange," said his father. "The wind's not in the east this morning, and it's only an east wind that could burst in your window. You can't have shut it properly."

"Yes, father, I did — the first time I shut it just as well as the second, and it didn't blow open after the second time. But I *know* I shut it well both times. I think it must be in the east, for it felt so sharp when it blew in."

"It must have changed quickly then," said the farmer, eyeing the sky through the large old-fashioned kitchen window in front of him. "That's the queer thing hereabouts; many a day if I was put to it to answer, I couldn't say which way the wind was blowing."

"Or which way it *wasn't* blowing, would be more like it," said Mrs. Conyfer with a smile. "It's to be hoped it'll blow you the right way to school anyway, Gratian. You don't look sure of it this morning!"

"I'm cold, mother, and I've always got to do what

I don't want. Last night I didn't want to go to bed, and this morning I didn't want to get up, and now I don't want to go to school, and I must."

He got up slowly and unwillingly and began putting his books together. His mother looked at him with a slight smile on her face.

"'Must''s a grand word, Gratian," she said. "I don't know what we'd be without it. You'll feel all right once you're scampering across the moor."

"Maybe," he replied. But his tone was rather plaintive still. He was feeling "sorry for himself" this morning.

Things in general, however, did seem brighter, as his mother had prophesied they would, when he found himself outside. It was really not cold after all; it was one of those breezy yet not chilly mornings when, though there is nothing depressing in the air, there is a curious feeling of mystery — as if nature were holding secret discussions, which the winds and the waves, the hills and the clouds, the trees and the birds even, know all about, but which we — clumsy creatures that we are — are as yet shut out from.

"What is it all about, I wonder?" said Gratian to himself, as he became conscious of this feeling — an *autumn* feeling it always is, I think. "Everything seems so grave. Are they planning about the winter coming, and how the flowers and all the tender little plants are to be taken care of till it is over? Or is there going to be a great storm up in the sky? perhaps they are trying to settle it without a battle, but it does look very gloomy up there."

For the grayness had the threatening steel-blue shade over it which betokens disturbance of some kind. Still the child's spirits rose as he ran; there was something reviving in the little gusts of moorland breeze that met him every now and then, and he forgot everything else in the pleasure of the quick movement and the glow that soon replaced the chilly feelings with which he had set out.

He had run a good way, when something white, or light-coloured, fluttering on the ground some little way before him, caught his eye. And as he drew nearer he saw that it was a book, or papers of some kind, hooked on to a low-growing furze bush. Suddenly the words of the mysterious figure of the night before returned to his mind — "Look for the furze bush on the right of the path where it turns for the last time," she had said.

Gratian stopped short. Yes — there in front of him was the landmark — the path turned here for the last time, as she had said. He looked about him in astonishment.

"This was where my books were last night, then," he said to himself. "I had no idea I had come so far! Why, I was home in half a second — it is very strange — I could fancy it was a dream, or else that last night and the rainbow dance *wasn't* a dream."

He ran on to where the white thing was still fluttering appealingly, as if begging him to detach it. Poor white thing! It was or had been an exercise-book. At first Gratian fancied it must be one of his copy-books, left behind by mistake after his fairy friend had given him back the rest of his books. But as soon as he took it in his hands and saw the neat, clear characters, he knew it was not his, and he did not need to look at the signature, " Anthony Ferris," to guess that it belonged to the miller's son — for Tony was a clever boy, almost at the head of the school, and famed for his very good writing.

" Ah ha," thought Gratian triumphantly, " I have you now, Master Tony."

He had recognised the book as containing Tony's dictation lessons, for here and there were the wrongly spelt words — not many of them, for Tony was a good speller too — marked by the schoolmaster.

" Tony must have meant to take the book home to copy it out clear, and correct the wrong spelling," thought Gratian. And he remembered hearing the teacher telling Tony's class that on the neatness with which this was done would depend several important good marks. " He'll not be head of his class, now he's lost this book. Serve him right for the trick he played me," said Gratian to himself, as he rolled up the tattered book and slipped it into his satchel. " It's not so badly torn but what he could have copied it out all right, but it would have been torn to pieces by this evening, now that the wind's getting up. So it isn't my fault but his own — nasty spiteful fellow. Where would all *my* poor books have been by now, thanks to him ?"

The wind was getting up indeed — and a cold biting wind too. For just as Gratian was thus thinking, there came down such a gust as he had but seldom felt the force of. For an instant he staggered and all but fell, so unprepared had he been for the sudden buffet. It took all his strength and agility to keep his feet during the short remainder of the moorland path, so sharp and violent were the blasts. And it was with face and hands tingling and smarting painfully that he entered the school-room.

CHAPTER V.

GOOD FOR EVIL.

TONY'S face was almost the first thing he caught sight of. It was not late, but several children were already there, and Tony, contrary to his custom, instead of playing outside till the very last moment, was in the schoolroom eagerly searching for something among the slates and books belonging to his class. Gratian understood the reason, and smiled to himself inwardly — but had he smiled visibly I don't think his face would have been improved by it. Nor was there real pleasure or rejoicing in the feeling of triumph which for a moment made him forget his smarting face and hands.

"How red you look, Gratian," said Dolly, Tony's sister, "have you been crying?"

"Crying — no, nonsense, Dolly," he replied in a tone such as gentle Gratian seldom used. "Whose face wouldn't be red with such a horrible wind cutting one to pieces."

"Wind!" repeated Dolly, "I didn't feel any wind.

It must have got up all of a sudden. Did you get home quickly last night?"

Gratian looked at her. For half an instant he wondered if there was any meaning in her question — had Dolly anything to do with the trick that had been played him? But his glance at her kindly, honest face reassured him. He was going to answer when Tony interrupted him.

"Got home quick," he said, looking up with a grin; "of course he did. He was in such a hurry to get to work. Didn't you see what a lot of books he took home with him? My! your shoulders must have ached before you got to the Farm, Gratian. Mine did, I know, though 'twas only a short bit I carried your satchel."

"It was pretty heavy," said Gratian, unfastening it as he spoke, and coolly taking out the books one after another, watching Tony the while, "but nothing to hurt. And I got all my lessons done nicely. It was kind of you, Tony, to help me to carry my satchel."

Tony stared — with eyes and mouth wide open.

"What's the matter?" said his sister. "You look as if you'd seen a ghost, Tony."

The boy turned away, muttering to himself.

"Tony's put out this morning," said Dolly in a low voice to Gratian, "and I can't help being sorry too. He's lost his exercise-book that he was to copy out clear — and the master said it'd have to do with getting the prize. Tony's in a great taking."

"How did he lose it?" asked Gratian with a rather queer feeling, as he wondered what Dolly would say if she knew that at that very moment the lost book was safely hidden away at the bottom of his satchel, which he took care not to leave within Tony's reach.

"He doesn't know," said Dolly dolefully. "He's sure he had it when we left school last night. We were looking for it all evening, and then he thought maybe it'd be here after all. But it isn't."

Then the bell rang for lessons to begin, and Gratian saw no more of Tony, who was at the other side of the schoolroom in a higher class, and though Dolly was in the same as himself, she was some places off, so that there was no chance of any talking or whispering.

Gratian's lessons were well learnt and understood. It was not long before he found himself higher in his class than he had almost ever done before, and he caught the master's eye looking at him with approval, and a smile of encouragement on his face. Why was it he could not meet it with a brightly answering smile as he would have done the day before? Why did he turn away, his cheeks tingling again as if the wind had been slapping them, here inside the sheltered schoolroom?

The master felt a little disappointed.

"He will never do really well if he is so foolishly shy and bashful," he said to himself, when Gratian turned away as if ashamed to be grateful for the few kinds words the teacher said to him at the end of the morning's lessons; and the boy, in a corner of the playground by himself when the other children had run home for their dinner, felt nearly, if not quite, as unhappy as the day before.

"I don't see why I should mind about Tony," he was thinking as he sat there. "He's a naughty, unkind boy, and he deserves to be punished. If it hadn't been for *her* helping me, I wouldn't have known my lessons a bit this morning, and the master would have thought I was never going to try. I just hope Tony will lose his place and the prize and everything. Oh, how cold it is!" for round the wall, *through* it indeed, it almost seemed, came sneaking a sharp little gust of air, so cold, so cutting, that Gratian actually shivered and shook, and the smarting in his face began again. "I feel cold even in my bones," he said to himself.

Just then voices reached his ear. The door of the schoolhouse opened and the master appeared, showing out a lady, who had evidently come to speak to him about something. She was a very pleasant-looking lady, and Gratian's eyes rested with satisfaction on her pretty dress and graceful figure.

"Then you will not forget about it? You will let me know in a few days what you think?" Gratian heard her say.

"Certainly, madam," replied the schoolmaster. "I have already one or two in my mind who, I think, may be suitable. But I should like to think it over and to ask the parents' consent."

"Of course — of course. Good-bye then for the present, and thank you," said the lady, and then she went out at the little garden-gate and the schoolmaster returned into his house.

"I wonder what they were talking about," thought Gratian. But he soon forgot all about it again — his mind was too full of its own affairs.

Tony looked vexed and unhappy that afternoon, and Dolly's rosy face bore traces of tears. She overtook Gratian on his way home in the evening, and began again talking about the lost book.

"It's so vexing for Tony, isn't it?" she said, "and do you know, Gratian, it's even more vexing than we thought. Did you see a lady at the school to-day? Do you know who she was?"

Gratian shook his head.

"She's the lady from the Big House down the road, that's been shut up so long. It isn't her house, but she's the sister or the cousin of the gentleman it belongs to, and he's lent it to her because the doctors said the air hereabouts would be good for her little boy. He's ill someway, he can scarcely walk. And she came to the school to-day to ask master if one of the boys — his best boy, she said — might go sometimes to play with her little boy and read to him a little. And Tony was sure of being the top of the class if only he had finished copying out those exercises — he'd put right all the faults the master had marked, and it only wanted copying. But now he's no chance; the other boys have theirs nearly done."

"How do you know about what the lady said?" Gratian asked.

"The master told mother. He met her in the village just before afternoon lessons, and asked her if she'd let Tony go, if so be as he was head of his class."

"And would he like to go, d'ye think, Dolly?" asked Gratian.

"He'd like to be head of his class, anyway," the sister replied. "I don't know as father can let him go, for we're very busy at the mill, and Tony's big enough to help when he's not at school. But he'd not like to see Ben or that conceited Robert put before him. If it were you now, Gratian, I don't think he'd mind so much."

Gratian's heart beat fast at her words. Visions of the pleasure of going to see the pretty lady and her boy, of hearing her soft voice speaking to him, and of seeing the inside of the Big House, which had always been a subject of curiosity to the children of the village, rose temptingly before him. But they soon faded.

"Me!" he exclaimed, "I'd have no chance — even failing Tony."

"I don't know," said Dolly. "You're never a naughty boy, and you can read very nice when you like. Master always seems to think you read next best to Tony. I shouldn't wonder if he sent you, if he's vexed with Tony. And he will be that, for he told him to do out that writing so very neatly. I think it was to be shown to the gentlemen that come to see the school sometimes. But I mustn't go any farther with you, Gratian. It'll be dark before I get home. I'm afraid Tony must have dropped the book out here, and that it blew away. Good-night, Gratian."

"Good-night, Dolly," he replied. And then after a little hesitation he added, "I wish — I wish Tony hadn't lost his book."

"Thank you, Gratian," said the little girl as she ran off.

Gratian stood and looked after her with a queer mixture of feelings. It was true, as he had said to Dolly, he did wish Tony had not lost his book, but almost more he wished *he* had not found it. But just now, standing there in the softly fading light, with the evening breeze — no longer the sharp blast of the morning — gently fanning his cheeks, looking after little Dolly as she ran home, and thinking of Tony's sunburnt troubled face, the angry feelings seemed to grow fainter, till the wish to see his schoolfellow punished for his mischievous trick died away altogether. And once he had got to this, it was a quick step to still better things.

"Look here, Dolly," and he held out to her the Poor Copy-Book which he had already taken out of his Satchel.—p. 57.

"I *will*, I *will*," he shouted out aloud, though there was no one — *was* there no one? — to hear. And as he sprang forward to rush after Dolly and overtake her, it seemed to him that he was half-lifted from his feet, and at the same moment another waft of the breeze he had been feeling, though still softer and with a scent as of spring flowers about it, blew into his face.

"Are you kissing me, kind wind?" he said laughing, and in answer, as it were, he felt himself blown along almost as swiftly as the night before. At this rate it did not take him long to gain ground on the miller's daughter.

"Dolly, Dolly," he called out when he saw himself within a few paces of her. "Stop, do stop. I have something for you — something to say to you."

Dolly turned round in astonishment.

"Gratian!" she exclaimed, "have you been running after me all this time? I would have waited for you if I'd known."

"Never mind. I ran very fast," said Gratian. "Look here, Dolly," and he held out to her the poor copy-book which he had already taken out of his satchel. "This is what I ran after you for; give it to Tony, and — "

"Tony's lost exercise-book!" cried Dolly. "Oh Gratian, how glad he will be. Where did you find it? *How* good of you! Did you find it just now, since you said good-night to me?"

Gratian's face grew red, but it was too dark for Dolly to see.

"No," he said, "I found it before. But — but — Tony had done me a bad turn, Dolly, and it wasn't easy — not all at once — to do him a good one instead. But I've done it now, and you may tell him what I say. I'm quite in earnest, and I'm glad I've done it. Tell him I hope he'll be the head of his class now, anyway, and — "

"Gratian," said Dolly, catching hold of his arm as she spoke, "I don't know what the trick was that Tony played you, or tried to play you. But I know he's terrible fond of tricks, though I don't think he's got a bad heart. And it was too bad of him to play it on you, it was — you that never does ill turns to none of us."

"I've been near it this time, though," said Gratian, feeling, now that the temptation was over, the comfort of confessing the worst. "I was very mad with Tony, and I didn't like bringing myself to give back his book. I don't want you to think me better than I am, Dolly."

"But I do think you very good all the same, I do," said the little girl earnestly, "and I'll tell Tony so. And you shan't have any more tricks played you by him — he's not so bad as that. Thank you very much, Gratian. If he gets the prize, it'll be all through you."

"And about going to the Big House," added

Gratian, rather sadly. "He'll be the one for that now. I think that's far before getting a prize. It was thinking of that made me feel I *must* give him his book. I'd give a good deal, I know, to be the one to go to the Big House."

"Would you?" said Dolly, a little surprised, for it was not very often Gratian spoke so eagerly about anything. "I don't know that I'd care so much about it. And to be sure you might have been the one if you hadn't helped Tony now! But I don't know that it would be much fun after all — just amusing a little boy that's ill."

"You didn't see the lady, Dolly, but *I* did," said Gratian. "She's not like any one I ever saw before — she's so beautiful. Her hair's a little the colour of yours, I think, but her skin's like — like cream, and her eyes are as kind as forget-me-nots."

"Was she finely dressed?" asked Dolly, becoming interested.

"Yes — at least I think so. Her dress was very soft, and a nice sort of shiny way when she moved, and she spoke so prettily. And oh, Dolly, it'd be terribly nice to see the Big House. Fancy, I've heard tell there are beautiful pictures there."

"Pictures — big ones in gold frames, do you mean?" Dolly inquired.

"I don't know about gold frames. I've never seen any. But pictures of all sorts of things — of places far away, I dare say, where the sky is so blue

and the big sea — like what the master tells us
sometimes in our geography. Oh, I'd like more than
anything to see pictures, Dolly."

"I never thought about such things. What a
funny boy you are, Gratian," said Dolly, as she ran
off joyfully, with Tony's tattered book in her hand.

It did not take Gratian long to make his way
home — the feeling of having done right "adds
feather to the heel." But as he sped along the
moorland path he could not help wondering to himself if his soft-voiced friend of the night before were
anywhere near.

"I think she must be pleased with me," he
thought. "It feels like her kissing me," as just then
the evening breeze again met him as he ran. "Is it
you Golden-wings, or you, Spirit of the Waves?" he
said, for he had learnt in his dream to think of them
thus. And a little soft laughter in the air about
him told him he was not far wrong. "Perhaps it
is both together," he thought. "I think they are
pleased. It is nicer than when that sharp East-wind
comes snapping at one — though after all, East-wind,
I think perhaps I should thank you for having stung
me as you did this morning — I rather think I
deserved it."

Whiz, rush, dash — came a sharp blast as he
spoke. Gratian started, and for half a moment felt
almost angry.

"I didn't deserve it just now, though," he said.

But a ripple of laughter above him made his vexation fade away.

"You silly boy," came a whisper close to his ear. "Can't you take a joke?"

"Yes, that I can, as well as any one;" and no sooner were the words out of his mouth than again, with the whir and the swoop now becoming familiar to him, he was once more raised from the ground, and really, before he knew where he was, he found himself at the gate of the farm-house.

His mother was just coming out to the door.

"Dear me, child," she said, "how suddenly you have come! I have been out several times to the gate to look for you, but though it is not yet dark I didn't see you."

"I did come very quickly, mother dear," said Gratian, and for a moment he thought of telling her about his strange new friends. But somehow, when he was on the point of doing so, the words would not come, and his feelings grew misty and confused as when one tries to recollect a dream that one knows was in one's memory but a moment before. And he felt that the voices of the winds were as little to be told as are the songs of the birds to those who have not heard them for themselves. So he just looked up in his mother's face with a smile, and she stooped and kissed him — which she did not very often do. For the moorland people are not soft and caressing in their ways, but rather sharp and rugged, though their hearts are true.

"I wonder where you come from, sometimes, Gratian," said his mother half-laughing. "You don't seem like the other children about."

"But mother, I'm getting over dreaming at my lessons. I am indeed," said the child brightly. "I think when you ask the master about me the next time, he'll tell you he's pleased with me."

"That's my good boy," said she well pleased.

So the day ended well for the child of the Four Winds.

CHAPTER VI.

ORGAN TONES.

As Gratian was running in to school the next morning he felt some one tugging at his coat, and looking round, there was Tony, his round face redder than usual, his eyes bright and yet shy.

"She give it me, Gratian — Doll did — and — and — I've to thank you. I was awful glad — I was that."

" Have you got it done ? Will it be all right for the prize and all that ?" asked Gratian.

Tony nodded.

" I think so. I sat up late last night writing, and I think I'll get it done to-night. It was awful good of you, Gratian," Tony went on, growing more at his ease, " for I won't go for to say that it wasn't a mean trick about the stones. But I meant to go back and get the books and keep them safe for you till the next morning. You did look so funny tramping along with the bag of stones," and Tony's face screwed itself up as if he wanted to laugh but dared not.

"It didn't *feel* funny," said Gratian. "It felt very horrid. Indeed it makes me get cross to think of it even now—don't say any more about it, Tony."

For it did seem to him as if, after all, the miller's boy was getting off rather easily! And it felt a little hard that all the good things should be falling to Tony's share, when he had been so unkind to another.

"I want to forget it," he went on; "if the master knew about it, he'd not let you off without a good scolding. But I'm not going to stand here shivering—I tell you I don't want to say any more about it, Tony."

"Shivering," repeated Tony, "why it's a wonderful mild morning for November. Father was just saying so"—and to tell the truth Gratian himself had thought it so as he ran across the moor. "But, Gratian, you needn't be so mad with me now—I know it was a mean trick, and just to show you that I know it, I promise you the master *shall* know all about it," and Tony held his head higher as he said the words. "There's only one thing, Gratian. I do wish you'd tell me where you found my book, and how you knew where I'd hidden yours? I've been thinking and thinking about it, and I can't make it out. Folks do say as there's still queer customers to be met on the moor after nightfall. I wonder if you got the fairies to help you, Gratian?" added Tony laughing.

Gratian laughed too.

"No, Tony, it wasn't the fairies," he said, his good-humour returning. And it was quite restored by a sweet soft whisper at that moment breathed into his ear — "no, not the fairies — but who it was is our secret — eh, Gratian?" And Gratian laughed again softly in return.

"Who was it then?" persisted Tony. But just then the school-bell rang, and there was no time for more talking.

Tony was kept very busy for the next day or two with his writing-out, which took him longer than he expected. Gratian too was working hard to make up for lost time, but he felt happy. He saw that the master was pleased, and that his companions were beginning to look up to him as they had never done before. But he missed his new friends. The weather was very still — for some days he had heard scarcely a rustle among the trees and bushes, and though he had lain awake at night, no murmuring voices in the chimney had reached his ears.

"Have they gone away already? Was it all a dream?" the child asked himself sadly.

Sunday came round again, and Gratian set off to church with his father and mother. Going to church was one of his pleasures — of late especially, for the owner of the Big House, though seldom there himself, was generous and rich, and he had spent money in restoring the church and giving a beautiful organ.

And on Sunday mornings an organist came from a distance to play on it, but in the afternoon its great voice was silent, for no one in the village — not even the schoolmaster, who was supposed to know most things — knew how to play on it. For this reason Gratian never cared to go to church the second time — he would much rather have stayed out on the moor with Jonas and Watch, and sometimes, in the fine summer weather, when the walk was hot and tiring even for big people, his mother had allowed him to do so. But now, with winter at hand, it was not fit for sauntering about or lying on the heather especially with Sunday clothes on, so the child knew it was no use asking to stay at home.

This Sunday afternoon brought a very welcome surprise. Scarcely was the boy settled in his corner beside his mother, before the rich deep tones fell on his ear. He started and looked about him, not sure if his fancy were not playing him false. But no — clearer and stronger grew the music — there was no mistake, and Gratian gave himself up to the pleasure of listening. And never had it been to him more beautiful. New fancies mingled with his enjoyment of it, for it seemed to him that he could distinguish in it the voices of his friends — the loving, plaintive breath of the west, telling of the lapping of the waves on some lonely shore; the sterner, deeper tones of the strong spirit of the north; even the sharply thrilling blast of the ever-restless east wind seemed to flash here and there like lightning darts, cutting through and yet melting again into the harmony. And then from time to time the sweet, rich glowing song of praise from the lips of Golden-wings, the joyful.

"Yes, they are all there," said Gratian to himself in an ecstasy of completest pleasure. "I hear them all. That is perhaps why they have not come to me lately — it was to be a surprise! But I have found you out, you see. Ah, if I could play on the organ you could never hide yourselves from me for long, my friends. Perhaps the organ is one of their real homes. I wonder if it can be."

And his face looked so bright and yet absorbed that his mother could not help smiling at him, as they sat waiting for a moment after the last notes had died away.

"Are you so pleased to have music in the afternoon too?" she said. "It is thanks to the stranger lady — the squire's cousin, who has come to the Big House. There — you can see her. She is just closing the organ."

Gratian stood up on his tiptoes and bent forward as far as he could. He caught but one glimpse of the fair face, but it was enough. It *was* the same — the lady with the forget-me-not eyes; and his own eyes beamed with fresh delight.

"They must be friends of hers too," was the first thought that darted through his brain; "she must know them, else she couldn't make their voices come like that. Oh dear, if I could but go to the Big House, perhaps she would tell me about how she knows them."

But even to think of the possibility was very nice. Gratian mused on it, turning it over and over in his mind, as was his wont, all the way home. And that evening, while he sat in his corner reading over the verses which the master always liked the scholars to say on the Monday morning — his father and mother with their big Sunday books open on the table before them as usual — a strange feeling came over him that he was again in the church, again listening to the organ; and so absorbing grew the feeling that, fearful of its vanishing, he closed his eyes and leaned his curly head on the wooden rail of the old chair and listened. Yes, clearer and fuller grew the tones — he was curled up in a corner of the chancel by this time, in his dream — and gradually in front, as it were, of the background of sound, grew out the voices he had learnt to know so well. They all seemed to be singing together at first, but by degrees the singing turned into soft speaking, the sound of the organ had faded into silence, and opening his eyes, by a faint ray of moonlight creeping in through the window, he saw he was in his own bed in his own room.

How had he come there? Had his mother carried him up and undressed him without awaking him as she had sometimes done when he was a very tiny boy?

"No — she couldn't. I'm too big and heavy," he thought sleepily. "But hush! the voices again."

"Yes, I carried him up. He was so sleepy — he never knew — nobody knew. The mother looked round and thought he had gone off himself. And Golden-wings undressed him. He will notice the scent on his little shirt when he puts it on in the morning."

"Humph!" replied a second voice, in a rather surly tone. "you are spoiling the child, you and our sister of the south. Snow-wings and I must take him in hand a while — a whi—ile."

For the East-wind was evidently in a hurry. Her voice grew fainter as if she were flying away.

"Stop a moment," said the softest voice of all. "It's not fair of you to say we are spoiling the child — Sea-breezes and I — we're doing nothing of the kind. We never pet or comfort him save when he deserves it — we keep strictly to our compact. You and our icy sister have been free to interfere when you thought right. Do you hear, Gray-wings? do you he—ar?"

And far off, from the very top of the chimney, came Gray-wing's reply.

"All right — all right, but I haven't time to wait. Good-night — go—od-ni—ight," and for once East-wind's voice sounded soft and musical.

Then the two gentle sisters went on murmuring together, and what they said was very pleasant to Gratian to hear.

"*I* say," said Golden-wings, — "*I* say he has been a very good boy. He is doing credit to his training, little though he suspects how long he has been under our charge."

"He is awaking to that and to other things now," replied she whom the others called the Spirit of the Sea. "It is sad to think that some day our guardianship must come to an end."

"Well, don't think of it, then. *I* never think of disagreeable things," replied the bright voice.

"But how can one help it? Think how tiny he was — the queer little red-faced solemn-eyed baby, when we first sang our lullabies to him, and how we looked forward to the time when he should hear more in our voices than any one but a godchild of ours *can* hear. And now —"

"Now that time has come, and we must take care what we say — he may be awake at this very moment. But listen, sister — I think we must do something — you and I. Our sterner sisters are all very well in their places, but all work and no play is not *my* idea of education. Now listen to my plan;" but here the murmuring grew so soft and vague that Gratian could no longer distinguish the syllables. He tried to strain his ears, but it was useless, and he grew sleepy through the trying to keep awake. The last sound he was conscious of was a flapping of wings and a murmured "Good-night, Gratian. Good-night, little godson — good-ni—ight," and then he fell asleep and slept till morning.

He would have forgotten it all perhaps, or remembered it only with the indistinctness of a dream that is past, had it not been for something unusual in the look of the little heap of clothes which lay on the chair beside his bed. They were so *very* neatly folded — though Gratian prided himself rather on his own neat folding — and the shirt was so snow-white and smooth that the boy thought at first his mother had laid out a fresh one while he was asleep. But no — yesterday was Sunday. Mrs. Conyfer would have thought another clean one on Monday very extravagant — besides, not even from her linen drawers, scented with lavender, could have come that delicious fragrance! Gratian snuffed and sniffed with ever-increasing satisfaction, as the words he had overheard in the night returned to his memory. And his stockings — they too were scented! What it was like I could not tell you, unless it be true, as old travellers say, that miles and miles away from the far-famed Spice Islands their fragrance may be perceived, wafted out to sea by the breeze. That, I think, may give you a faint idea of the perfume left by the South-wind on her godson's garments.

"So it's true — I wasn't dreaming," thought the boy. "I wonder what the plot was that I couldn't hear about. I shall know before long, I dare say."

At breakfast he noticed his mother looking at him curiously.

"What is it, mother?" he said; "is my hair not neat?"

"No, child. On the contrary, I was thinking how very tidy you look this morning. Your collar is so smooth and clean. Can it be the one you wore yesterday?"

"Yes, mother," he replied, "just look how nice it is. And hasn't it a nice scent?"

He got up as he spoke and stood beside her. She smoothed his collar with satisfaction.

"It is certainly very well starched and ironed," she said. "Madge is improving; I must tell her so. That new soap too has quite a pleasant smell about it—like new-mown hay. It's partly the lavender in the drawers, I dare say."

But Gratian smiled to himself—thinking he knew better!

"Gratian," said his mother, two mornings later, as he was starting for school, "I had a message from the master yesterday. He wants to see me about you, but he is very busy, and he says if father or I should be in the village to-day or to-morrow, he would take it kindly if we would look in. I must call at the mill for father to-day—he's too busy to go himself—so I think I'll go on to school, and then we can walk back together. So don't start home this afternoon till I come."

“No, mother, I won’t,” said Gratian. But he still hung about as if he had more to say.

“What is it?” asked his mother. “You’re not afraid the master’s going to give a bad account of you?”

“No, mother—not since I’ve cured myself of dreaming,” he answered. “I was only wondering if I knew what it was he was going to ask you.”

“Better wait and know for sure,” said his mother. So Gratian set off.

But he found it impossible not to keep thinking and wondering about it to himself. Could it be anything about the Big House? Had Tony kept his promise, and told the master of the trick he had played, so that Gratian, and not he, should be chosen?

“He didn’t seem to care about it much,” thought Gratian, “not near so much as I should—oh, dear no! Still it wouldn’t be very nice for him to have to tell against himself, whether he cared about it or not.”

But as his mother had said, it was best to wait a while and know, instead of wasting time in fruitless guessing.

Tony seemed quite cheerful and merry, and little Dolly was as friendly as possible. After the morning lessons were over and the other children dispersed, the schoolmaster called Gratian in again.

“It is too cold now for you to eat your dinner in

the playground, my boy," he said. " After you have run about a little, come in and find a warmer dining-room inside. But I have something else to say to you. I had a talk with Anthony Ferris yesterday."

Gratian felt himself growing red, but he did not speak.

" He told me of the trick he'd played you. A very unkind and silly trick it was, and so I said to him; but as he told it himself I won't punish him. He told me more, Gratian — of your finding his book and giving it back to him, when you might have done him an ill turn by keeping it."

" I did keep it all one day, sir," said Gratian humbly.

" Ah well, you did give it him in the end," said the master smiling. " I am pleased to see that you did the right thing in face of temptation. And Tony feels it himself. He's an honest-hearted lad and a clever one. He has done that piece of work I gave him well, and no doubt he stands as the head boy" — here the master stopped and seemed to be thinking over something. Then he went on again rather abruptly.

" That was all I wanted to say to you just now, I think. Tony is really grateful to you, and if he can show it, he will. Did your father or mother say anything about coming to see me ?"

" Please, sir, mother's coming this afternoon. I'm to wait and go home with her."

" Ah well, that's all right."

But Gratian had plenty to think of while he ate his dinner. He was very much impressed by Tony's having really told.

" I wonder," he kept saying to himself, " I do wonder if perhaps — "

CHAPTER VII.

THE BIG HOUSE AND THE LADY.

MRS. CONYFER was waiting for Gratian at the gate of the schoolhouse when he came out.

"We must make haste," she said; "I think it's going to rain."

Gratian looked up at the sky, and sniffed the cold evening air.

" Yes," he said, "I think it is."

"It's not so cold quite as it was when I came down," Mrs. Conyfer went on—the dwellers at Four Winds often spoke of "coming down," when they meant going to the village—"that's perhaps because the rain is coming. I don't want to get my bonnet spoilt — I might have known it was going to rain when father said the wind was in the west."

"Why does the west wind bring rain?" asked Gratian; " is it because it comes from the sea?"

"Nay," said his mother, "I don't know. You should know better about such things than I — you that's always listening to the winds and hearing what they've got to say."

Gratian looked up, a little surprised.

"What makes you say that, mother?" he asked.

Mrs. Conyfer laughed a little.

"I scarcely know," she said. "We always said of you when you were a baby that you seemed to hear words in the wind — you were always content to lie still, no matter how long you were left, if only the wind were blowing. And it seems to me even now that you're always happiest and best when there's wind about, though it's maybe only a fancy of mine."

But Gratian looked pleased.

"No, mother," he said, "I don't think it's a fancy. I think myself it's quite true."

And he pulled off his cap as he spoke and let the wind blow his hair about, and lifted up his face as if inviting its caresses.

"It's getting up," he said. "But I think we'll get home before the rain comes."

His mother had not heard the whisper that had reached his ear through the gust of wind.

"I will help you home, Gratian, both you and your mother, though she won't know it."

He laughed to himself when he felt the gentle, steady way in which they were blown along — never had the long walk to the Farm seemed so short to Mrs. Conyfer.

"Dear me," she said, when they were within a few yards of the gate, "I couldn't have believed we were home! It makes a difference when the wind is with us, I suppose."

Gratian pulled her back a moment, as she was going in.

"Mother," he said, "what was it the master wanted to say to you? Won't you tell me?"

"I must speak first to father," she replied; "it's something which we must have his leave for first."

Gratian could not ask any more, and nothing more was said to him till the next morning when he was starting for school. Then his mother came to the door with him.

"I've a message for the master," she said. "Listen, Gratian. You must tell him from me that father and I have no objection to his doing as he likes about what he spoke to me of yesterday. He said he'd like to tell you about it himself — so I won't tell you any more. Maybe you'll not care about it when you hear it."

"Ah — I don't think that," said the boy, as he ran off.

He needed no blowing to school that morning. The way seemed short, even though it was still drizzling — a cold, disagreeable, small rain, which had succeeded the downpour of the night before. But Gratian cared little for rain — what true child of the moors could? — he rather liked it than otherwise, especially when it came drifting over in great sheets, almost blinding for the moment, and then again

dispersed as suddenly, so that standing on the high
ground one could see on the slopes beneath when
it was raining and when it stopped. It gave one a
feeling of being "above the clouds" that Gratian
liked. But this morning there was nothing of a
weather panorama of that kind — just sheer, steady,
sapping rain, with no wind to interfere.

"They are tired, I dare say," thought Gratian;
"for they must have been hard at work last night,
getting the clouds together for all this rain. I
expect Golden-wings goes off altogether when it's
so cold and dreary. I wonder where she is. I would
like to see her home — it must be full of such beautiful colours and scents."

"And mine — wouldn't you like to see mine?"
whistled a sudden cold breath in his ear. "Yes, I
have made you jump. But I'm not going to bring
the snow just yet — I've just come down for a
moment, to see how much rain Green-wings has got
together. She mustn't waste it, you see. I can't
have her interfering with my reservoirs for the
winter. I hold with a good old-fashioned winter —
a snowy Christmas and plenty of picture exhibitions
for my pet artist, Jack Frost. A good winter's the
healthiest in the end for all concerned."

"Yes, I think so to," said Gratian. He wished
to be civil to White-wings. It was interesting to
have some one to talk to as he went along, and the
North-wind in a mild mood seemed an agreeable

companion, less snappish and jerky than her sister of the east.

"That's a sensible boy," said the snow-bringer condescendingly; "you've something of the old northern spirit about you here on the moorlands still, I fancy. Ah! if you could see the north — the real north — I don't fancy you would care much about the sleepy golden lands you were dreaming of just now."

"I'd like to *see* them," replied the child; "I don't say I'd like to live in them always. But the scents and the colours — they must be very beautiful. I seem to know all about them when Golden-wings kisses me."

"Humph," said the Spirit of the North. Both she and Gray-wings had a peculiar way of saying "humph" when Gratian praised either of the gentler sisters — "as for scents I don't say — scent is a stupid sort of thing. I don't understand anything about it. But *colours* — you're mistaken, I assure you, if you think the south can beat me in that. You've got your head full of the idea of snow — interminable ice-fields and all the rest of it. Why, my good boy, did you never here of Arctic sunsets — not to speak of the Northern Lights? I could show you sunsets and sunrises such as you have never dreamt of — like rainbows painted on gold. Ah, it is a pity you cannot come with me!"

"And why can't I?" asked Gratian. "I'm not afraid of the cold."

The North-wind gave a whistle of good-natured contempt.

"My dear, you'd have no time to be afraid or not afraid — you'd be dead before you'd even looked about you. Ah — it's a terrible inconvenience, those bodies of yours — if you were like *us*, now! But I mustn't waste my time talking, only as I was passing I thought I'd say a word or two. When my sisters are all together there's never any getting in a syllable edgeways. Good-bye, my child. We'll meet again oftener during the next few months."

"Good-bye, Godmother White-wings," said Gratian, and a gust of wind rushing past him with a whistle seemed to answer, "Good-bye."

"I'm very glad to have had a little talk with her," he said to himself; "she's much nicer than I thought she was, and she makes one feel so strong and brisk. Dear me — what wonderful places there must be up in the north where she lives!"

The master called him aside after morning lessons.

"Did your mother send any message to me, Gratian?" he asked.

"Yes, sir," and he repeated what Mrs. Conyfer had said.

The schoolmaster looked pleased.

"I'm glad she and your father have no objection," he said. "I think it may be a good thing for you in several ways. But I must explain it to you. You know the Big House as they call it, here? A lady

and her son have come to stay there for a time—
relations of the squire's—"

"Yes, sir, I know," interrupted Gratian; "she
plays the organ on Sunday afternoons, and her little
boy is ill."

"Not exactly ill, but he had a fall, and he mustn't
walk about or stand much. It's dull for him, as at
home he was used to companions. His mother asked
me to send him one of my best boys—a boy who
could read well for one thing—as a playmate. At
first I thought of Tony Ferris, and I spoke of him.
But Tony has begged me to choose you instead of
him."

Gratian raised his brown eyes and fixed them on
the master's face.

"Does Tony not want to go?" he asked. "I
shouldn't like to take it from him if he wants to go."

"I think he would be happier for you to go," said
the master, "and perhaps you may be more suitable.
Besides Tony thinks that he owes you something.
He has told me of the trick he played you, as you
know—and certainly you deserve to be chosen more
than he. I am not sure that he would care much
about it; but still it will give him pleasure to think
he has got it for you, and we may let him have this
pleasure."

"Yes, sir," said Gratian thoughtfully. And then
he added, "it was good of Tony to ask for it for me."

"Yes, it was," agreed the master.

"Then when am I to go?" asked Gratian.

"This afternoon. I will let you off an hour or so earlier, and you can stay at the Big House till it is dark. It is no farther home from there than from here, if you go by the road at the back of it. We shall see how you get on, and then the lady will tell you about going again."

Gratian still lingered.

"What is it?" said the master. "Do you not think you shall like it?"

"Oh no, sir, oh no," exclaimed the child. "I was only wondering. Are there pictures at the Big House, do you think, sir?"

"Yes, I think there are some. Are you fond of pictures?"

"I don't know, sir. I've never seen any real ones. But I've often thought about them, and fancied them in my mind. There are such lots of things I'd like to see pictures of that I can't see any other way."

"Well, perhaps you will see some at the Big House," said the master with a smile.

Out in the playground Gratian ran against Tony.

"Has he told you?" he asked eagerly.

"Yes," said Gratian. "I'm to go this afternoon. It was very good of you, Tony, to want me to go instead of you."

Tony got rather red.

"I don't know that I'd a-cared about it much, Gratian," he said. "It wasn't that as cost me much.

But to tell you the truth, I did want to get out of telling the master about the trick I'd played you. And I don't know as I'd have told it, but a mighty queer thing happened — it's thanks to that I told."

"What was it?" asked Gracian.

"It was at night after I was in bed. I'd put off telling, and I thought maybe it'd all be forgotten. And that night all of a sudden there came such a storm of wind that it woke me up — the window had burst open, and I swear to you, Gratian — I've not told any one else — I saw a figure all in white, and with white wings, leaning over my bed, as if it had brought the storm with it. I was so frightened I began to think of all the bad things I had done, and I hollered out, 'I'll tell master first thing to-morrow morning, I will.' And with that the wind seemed to go down as sudden as it came, and I heard a sort of singing, something like when the organ plays very low in church, and there was a beautiful sweet scent of flowers through the room; and I suppose I fell asleep again, for when I woke it was morning, and I could have fancied it was all a dream, for nobody else had heard the wind in the night."

"We hear it most nights up at our place," said Gratian, "but I'm never frightened of it."

"You would have been that night — leastways I was. I durstn't go back from my word, dream or no dream — so now you know, Gratian, how I came to tell. And I hope you'll enjoy yourself at the Big House."

"I shall thank you for it if I do, all the same, Tony," Gratian replied.

"It's more in your way than mine. I'd feel myself such a great silly going among gentry folk like that," said Tony, as he scampered off to his dinner.

About three o'clock that afternoon Gratian found himself at the gates of the Big House. He had often passed by that way and stood looking in, but he had never been within the gates, for they were always kept locked; and there had been a strange, almost sad look of loneliness and desertedness about the place, even though the gardens had not been allowed to be untidy or overrun. Now it looked already different; the padlock and chain were removed, and there were the marks of wheels upon the gravel. It seemed to Gratian that even if he had not known there were visitors in the old house he would have guessed it.

He walked slowly up the avenue which led from the gates to the house. He was not the least afraid or shy, but he was full of interest and expectation. He wanted to see everything — to miss nothing, and even the walk up the avenue seemed to him full of wonder and charm. It *had* a charm of its own no doubt, for at each side stood pine-trees like rows of sentinels keeping guard on all comers, tall, stately, and solemn, only now and then moving their heads with silent dignity, as if in reply to observations passing among them up there, too high to be heard. The pines round Gratian's home were not so tall or straight—naturally, for they had a great deal of buffeting to do in order to live at all, and this of course did not help them to grow tall or erect. Gratian looked up in wonder at the great height.

"How I wish I knew what they say to each other up there," he said.

But just then a drop of something cold falling on his face made him start. It was beginning to rain.

"I wouldn't like to be wet when I first see the lady and the young gentleman," he thought. "I must be quick."

So off he set at a run, which perhaps did not much hasten matters, for when he got to the hall door he was so out of breath that he had to stand still for several minutes before venturing to ring.

The bell, when he did ring it, sounded sharp and hollow, almost like a bell ringing in an empty house. And when the door was opened, he saw that the large hall did look bare and empty, and he felt a little disappointed. But this feeling did not last long. Before he had time to say anything to the servant, a sweet, bright voice came sounding clearly.

"Oh, here he is, Fergus," were the words she said, and in another instant the owner of the voice appeared. It was the lady of the organ. She came forward smiling, and holding out her hand, but Gratian gazed at her for a moment without speaking, nor seeming to understand that she was speaking to him. He had never seen any one like her before. She was tall and fair, and her face was truly lovely. But what made it so, more than the delicate features or the pretty soft colours, was its sunny brightness, which yet from time to time was veiled by a look of pitying sadness, almost sweeter. And at these times the intense blueness of her eyes grew paler and fainter, so that they looked almost gray, like the sea when a cloud comes over the sunny sky above; only as Gratian had never seen the sea, he could not think this to himself.

What he did say to himself told it quite as well.

"She is like Golden-wings and Green-wings mixed together," was his thought.

And then having decided this, his mind seemed to grow clearer, the sort of confused bewilderment he had felt for a moment wafted itself away, and he distinguished the words she had repeated to him more than once.

"You are the little boy, Mr. Cornelius has kindly sent to see my poor little boy. It is kind too of you to come. I hope you and Fergus will be great friends."

She thought he was shy when at first he did not answer. But looking at him again she saw that it was not shyness which was speaking out of his big brown eyes.

"You are not afraid of me, are you?" she said smiling again.

"Oh no," he replied. "I didn't mean to be rude. I couldn't be frightened of you. I was only thinking — I never saw anybody so beautiful as you before," he went on simply, "and it made me think."

The lady flushed a little — a very little.

"I am pleased that you like my face," she said. "I like yours too, and I am sure Fergus will. Will you come and see him now? He is waiting eagerly for you."

She held out her hand again, and Gratian this time put his little brown one into it confidingly. And thus she led him out of the large, cold hall, down a short passage, rendered light and cheerful by a large window — here a door stood open, and a glow of warmth seemed to meet them as they drew near it.

CHAPTER VIII.

LITTLE FERGUS.

FOR there was a bright fire burning in the room, which sent red rays flickering and dancing in all directions, lighting up the faded tints of the ancient curtains and covers, and bringing rich crimson shades out of the shining, old dark mahogany furniture. There were flowers too; a bouquet of autumn leaves — bronze and copper and olive — with two or three fragile " last roses " in the middle, on which Gratian's eyes rested with pleasure for a moment, on their way to the small figure — the most interesting object of all.

He was lying on a little sofa, placed so as to be within reach of the fire's warmth, and yet near enough to the window for him to see out into the garden, to watch the life of the birds and the plants, the clouds and the breezes. The autumn afternoon looked later and darker now to Gratian as he glanced at it from within than when he was himself a part of it out-of-doors, and his eyes returned with pleasure to the nearer warmth and colour, though after the first momentary glimpse of the boy on the sofa a sort of shyness had made him look away.

For the child was extremely pale and thin — he looked much more ill than Gratian had been prepared for, and this gave him a feeling of timidity that nothing else could have caused. But the lady soon put him at his ease.

"Fergus, dear," she said, "here is the little friend you have been hoping for. Come over here near us, my dear boy"— for she had sat down on a low chair beside the couch, evidently her usual place —"and I will help you to get over the first few steps of making friends. To begin with," she said smiling, "do you know we don't know your name? That seems absurd, doesn't it? And you don't know ours."

"Yes — I know *his*," said Gratian, smiling too, and with a little gesture towards the invalid, so gentle and half-timid that no one could have called it rude; "you have just said it — Fergus. I never heard that name before."

"It is a Scotch name," said the lady. "One can almost fancy oneself in Scotland here. And tell us your name."

"Gratian," he replied, "Gratian Conyfer."

"What a nice name," said Fergus, speaking for the first time, "and what a queer one! I can say the same to you as you said to me, Gratian — I never heard that name before."

"How did you come by it?" asked Fergus's mother.

"I think it was because mother is called Grace, and there were several baby brothers that died, that were called for father," he replied.

"And how old are you?" asked Fergus, raising himself a little on his elbow. "I'm eight and a half. I'm not so very small for my age when I stand up — am I, mother?"

"No, dear," she answered with a little shadow over her bright face. "And you, Gratian?"

"I am nine," he said; "but they say at school I don't look so much. Tony is twelve, but he is much, much bigger."

"Tony — who is Tony?" asked Fergus; "is he your brother?"

"Oh no, I have no brothers. He's the head boy at the school."

"Yes," said Fergus's mother, "I remember about him. He was the boy Mr. Cornelius first thought of sending."

"And why didn't he come?" asked Fergus.

Gratian looked up at the lady.

"Did the master tell you?" he asked. The lady smiled, and nodded her head.

"Yes," she said, "I know the story. You may tell it to Fergus, Gratian; he would like to hear it. Now I am going away, for I have letters to write. In half an hour or so you shall have your tea. Would you like it here or in the library, Fergus?"

"Oh. in the library," he said eagerly. "I haven't been there for two days, mother. And then Gratian can see the pictures—you told me he liked pictures? —and best of all, you can play the organ to us, little mother."

"Then you feel better to-day, my boy?" she said, stooping to kiss the white forehead as she was leaving the room. "Some days I can't get him to like to move about at all." she added to Gratian.

"Yes, I do feel better," he said. "I don't mind it hurting me when I don't feel that horrible way as if I didn't care for *anything*. Have you ever been ill, Gratian? Do you know how it feels?"

Gratian considered.

"I once had a sore throat." he said, "but I didn't mind very much. It was winter. and I had a fire in my room. and I liked to see the flames going dancing up the chimney."

"Yes." said Fergus. "I know how you mean. I'm sure we must have the same thinkings about things. Gratian. Do you like music too, as much as pictures? Mother says people who like pictures very much. often like music too. and —and — there's something else that those kind of people like too, but I forget what."

"Flowers," suggested Gratian ; "flowers and trees, perhaps."

"No," said Fergus. looking a little puzzled, "these would count in with pictures, don't you think? I'll ask mother — she said it so nicely. Don't you like when anybody says a thing so that it seems to fit in with other things?"

"Yes," said Gratian, "I think I do. But I think things to myself, mostly — I've not got anybody much to talk to, except sometimes Jonas. He's got very nice thoughts, only he'd never say them except to Watch and me."

"Who's Watch?" asked Fergus eagerly. "Is he a dog?"

"He's our sheep-dog, and Jonas is the shepherd," replied Gratian. "They're sometimes alone with the sheep for days and days — out on the moors. It's so strange — I've been with them sometimes — it's like another world — to see the moors all round, ever so far, like the sea, I suppose — only I've never seen the sea — and not a creature anywhere, except some wild birds sometimes."

"Stop," said Fergus, closing his eyes; "yes, I can see it now. Go on, Gratian — is the sky gray, or blue with little white clouds?"

"Gray just now," said the boy, "and there's no wind that you can feel blowing. But it's coming -- you know it's coming — now and then Watch pricks up his ears, for he can tell it much farther off than we can, and old Jonas pats him a little. Jonas has an old blue round cap — a shepherd's cap — and his face is browny-red, but his hair is nearly white, and his eyes are very blue. Can you see him, Fergus?

And the sheep keep on browsing — they make a little scrumping noise when you are quite, quite close to them. And just before the wind really comes a great bird gives a cry — up, very high up — and it swoops down for a moment and then goes up again, till it looks just a little black speck against the sky. And all the time you know the wind is coming. Can you see it all, Fergus?"

"All," said the boy; "it's beautiful. You must tell me pictures often, Gratian, till I can go out again. I never had any one who could make them come so, except mother's music — they come with that. Haven't you noticed that they come with music?"

"I don't know," said Gratian. "I've never seen any real pictures — painted ones in big gold frames."

"There are some here," said Fergus; "not very many, but some. I like a few of them — perhaps you will too. But I like the pictures that come and go in one's fancy best. That's the kind that mother's music brings me."

"Yes," said Gratian, his eyes sparkling, "I understand."

"I was sure you would," said Fergus, with a tiny touch of patronising in his tone, which Gratian was too entirely single-minded to see, or rather perhaps to object to if he did see it. "I knew the minute I saw you, you'd suit me. I'm very glad that other fellow didn't come instead of you. But, by the bye, you haven't told me about that — mother said you'd tell me."

Gratian related the story of his satchel of stones. Fergus was boy enough to laugh a little, though he called it a mean trick ; but when Gratian told of having found his books again, he looked puzzled.

" How could you find them ? " he asked. " It was nearly dark, didn't you say ? "

" I don't quite know," replied Gratian, and he spoke the truth. It was always difficult for him to distinguish between real and fancy, dreaming and waking, in all concerning his four friends, and in some curious way this difficulty increased so much if he ever thought of talking about them, that he felt he was not meant to do so. " I have fancies some- times — like dreams, perhaps — that I can't explain. And they help me often — when I am in any trouble they help me."

" I don't see how fancies can help you to find things that are lost," said Fergus, who, except in his own particular way, was more practical that Gratian, "unless you mean that you dream things, and your dreams come true."

" It's a little like that," Gratian replied. " I think I had a sort of dream about coming here. I did so want to come — most of all since I heard the lady play in church."

" Yes," said Fergus, " isn't mother's playing beau- tiful ? I've not heard her play in church for ever so long, but I'm so glad there's an organ here. She plays to me every day. I like music best of everything in the world — don't you?"

To which Gratian gave his old answer — "I don't know yet."

Then they began talking of more commonplace things. Each told the other of his daily life and all his childish interests. Fergus was greatly struck by the account of Gratian's home — the old house with the queer name.

"How I should like to see it," he said, "and to feel the wind blow."

"The winds," corrected Gratian, "the four winds."

"The *four* winds," repeated Fergus. "North, south, east, and west. They don't blow all together, do they?"

"I think they do sometimes. Yes, I know they do — at night I'm sure I've heard them all four together, like tones in music."

Fergus looked delighted.

"Ah, you have to come back to music, you see," he said. "There's nothing tells everything and explains everything as well as music."

"You must have thought about it a great deal," said Gratian admiringly. "I've only just begun to think about things, and I think it's very puzzling, though I'm older than you. I don't know if music would explain things to me."

"Perhaps not as much as to me," said Fergus. "You see it's been my best thing — ever since I was five years old I've been lying like this. At home the others are very kind, but they can't quite understand," he added, shaking his head a little sadly: "they can all run about and jump and play. And when children can do all that, they don't need to think much. Still it is very dull without them — that is why I begged mother to try to get me somebody to play with. But I think you're better than that, Gratian. I think you understand more — how is it? You've never been ill or had to lie still."

"No," said the boy, "but I've had no brothers and sisters to play with me. And perhaps it's with being born at Four Winds — mother says so herself."

"I dare say it is," said Fergus gravely.

"Won't you get better soon?" asked Gratian, looking at Fergus with profound sympathy. For, gentle as he was, the idea of having to lie still, not being able to run about on the moors and feel his dear winds on his face, having even to call to others to help him before he could get to the window and look out on the sunshine — it seemed perhaps more dreadful to Gratian than it would have done to an ordinary, healthy child like Tony Ferris. "Won't you too be able to walk and run about — even if it's only a little?"

"I hope so," Fergus replied. "Mother says I mustn't expect ever to be quite strong. But they say I'm getting better. That's why mother brought me here. Do you know I can eat ever so much more than when I came? If I can get well enough to play — even on a piano — I wouldn't mind so much. I could make up all sorts of things for myself then — I could make pictures even of the moorland and Four Winds Farm, I think, Gratian."

"I'll try to tell you them — I'll try to make some of my fancies into stories and pictures," said Gratian; "then afterwards, when you get well and can play, you can make them into music."

Just then the door opened, and Fergus's mother came in.

"Tea is ready," she said, "and Andrew is going to carry you into the library, Fergus."

She looked at the boy a little anxiously as she spoke, and Gratian saw that a slight shadow of pain or fear crept over Fergus's face.

"Mother," he said, "would it perhaps be better to stay here after all? You could show Gratian the pictures."

The lady looked very disappointed.

"The tea is so nicely set out," she said, "and you know you can't hear the organ well from here. And Andrew doesn't hurt you — he is very careful."

Gratian looked on, anxious too. He understood that it must be good for Fergus to go into another room, otherwise his mother would not wish it. Fergus caught sight of the eagerness on Gratian's face, and it carried the day.

"I will go," he said; "here, Andrew."

A man-servant, with a good-humoured face and a strong pair of arms, came forward and lifted the child carefully.

"You walk beside me, Gratian, and hold my hand. If it hurts much I will pinch you a little, but don't let mother know," he said in a whisper: and thus the little procession moved out of the room right across the hall and down another corridor.

"There must be a window open," said Fergus; "don't you feel the air blowing in? Oh, don't shut it, mother," as the lady started forward, "it's such nice soft air — scented as if they were making hay. Oh, it's delicious."

His mother seemed a little surprised.

"There is no window open, dear," she said. "It must be that you feel the change from the warm room to the hall. Perhaps I should have covered you up."

"Oh no, no," repeated Fergus. "I'm not the least cold. It's not a cold wind at all. Gratian, don't *you* feel it?"

"Yes," said Gratian, holding Fergus's hand firmly. But his eyes had a curious look in them, as if he were smiling inwardly to himself.

"Golden-wings, you darling," he murmured, "I know you're there — thank you so much for blowing away his pain."

In another moment Fergus was settled on a couch

in the library — a lofty room with rows and rows of books on every side, nearly up to the ceiling. It would have looked gloomy and dull but for the cheerful fire in one corner and the neat tea-table drawn up before it; as it was, the sort of solemn mystery about it was very pleasing to Gratian.

" Isn't it nice here? " said Fergus. " I'm so glad I came. And do you know it didn't hurt me a bit. The fresh air that came in seemed to blow the pain away."

" I think you really must be getting stronger," said his mother, with a smile of hopefulness on her face, as she busied herself with the tea-table; "you have brought us good luck, Gratian."

" I believe he has," said Fergus. " Mother, do you know what he has been telling me? He was born where the four winds meet — he *must* be a lucky child, mustn't he, mother?"

" I should say so, certainly," said the lady with a smile. " I wonder if it is as good as being born on a Sunday."

" Oh far better, mother," said Fergus; " there are lots of children born on Sundays, but I never heard of one before that was born at the winds' meeting-place."

" Gratian will be able to tell you stories, I dare say," said his mother — " stories which the winds tell him, perhaps — eh, Gratian?"

Gratian smiled.

" He has been telling me some pictures already."
said Fergus; "oh. mother, I'm so happy."

" My darling," said his mother. " Now let me see
what a good appetite you have. You must be hungry too, Gratian, my boy. You have a long walk
home before you. "

Gratian was hungry. but he hardly felt as if he
could eat — there was so much to look at and to
think about. Everything was so dainty and pretty;
though he was well accustomed at the Farm to the
most perfect cleanliness and neatness, it was new to
him to see the sparkling silver. the tea-kettle boiling
on the spirit-lamp with a cheerful sound. the pretty
china and glass, and the variety of bread and cakes
to tempt poor Fergus's appetite. And the lady herself — with her forget-me-not eyes and sweet voice.
Gratian felt as if he were in fairyland.

CHAPTER IX.

MUSIC AND COUNSEL.

After tea Fergus's mother turned to the two boys.

"Shall I play to you now?" she said, "or shall we first show Gratian the pictures?"

"Play the last thing, please," said Fergus. "I like to keep it in my mind when I go to bed — it makes me sleep better. We can go into the gallery now and show Gratian the pictures; it would be too dark if we waited."

"It is rather dark already," said the lady, "still Gratian can see some, and the next time he comes he can look at them again."

She rang the bell, and when Andrew came, she told him to wheel Fergus's couch into the picture-gallery, which opened into the library where they were.

Andrew opened a double door at the other end of the room from that by which they had come in, and then he gently wheeled forward the couch on which Fergus was lying, and pushed it through the doorway. The gallery was scarcely large enough to deserve the name, but to Gratian's eyes it looked a very wonderful place. It was long and rather narrow and the light came from the top, and along the sides and ends were hung a good many pictures. All down one side were portraits — gentlemen with wigs, and ladies with powder, and some in queer, fancy dresses, mostly looking stiff and unnatural, though among them were some beautiful faces, and two or three portraits of children, which caught Gratian's eye.

"What do you think of them?" asked Fergus.

Gratian hesitated.

"I don't think people long ago could have been as pretty as they are now," he said at last. "except that lady in the long black dress — oh, she is very pretty, and so is the red little boy with the dog, and the two girls blowing soap-bubbles. The big one has got eyes like — like the lady's," he added half-timidly.

The lady looked pleased.

"You have a quick eye, Gratian," she said. "The pictures you admire are the best here, and that little girl is my great-grandmother. Now, look at the other side. These are pictures of all kinds — not family ones."

Gratian followed her in silence. The pictures were

mostly landscapes —some so very old and dark that one could scarcely distinguish what they were. And some of which the colours were brighter, the boy did not care for any better — they were not like any skies or trees he had ever seen or even imagined, and he felt disappointed.

Suddenly he gave a little cry.

" Oh, I like that — I do like that," he said, and he glanced up at the lady for approval.

She smiled again.

" Yes," she said, "it is a wonderful picture. Quite as much a picture of the wind as of the sea."

Gratian gazed at it with delight. The scene was on the coast, on what one might call a playfully stormy day. The waves came dancing in, their crests flashing in the sunshine, pursued and tossed by the wind: and up above, the little clouds were scudding along quite as busy and eager about *their* business, whatever it was, as the white-sailed fishing-boats below.

" Do you like it so very much?" she asked.

" Yes," the boy replied. " that's like what I fancied pictures were. I've never seen the sea, but I can feel it must be like that."

And after this he did not seem to care to see any others.

Fergus too was getting a little tired of lying alone while his mother and Gratian made the tour of the gallery. So Andrew was called to wheel him back

AND WHEN SHE SAT DOWN TO PLAY, THE LIGHT SPARKLED AND GLOWED
ON HER FAIR HAIR, MAKING IT LOOK LIKE GOLD. — p. 105.

again to the other door of the library, from whence he could best hear the organ. It stood at one side of the large hall, in a recess which had probably been made on purpose. It was dark in the recess even at mid-day, and now the dusk was fast increasing, so the lady lit the candles fixed at each side of the music-desk, and when she sat down to play the light sparkled and glowed on her fair hair, making it look like gold.

Gratian touched Fergus.

"Doesn't it look pretty?" he said, pointing to the little island of light in the gloomy hall.

Fergus nodded.

"I always think mother turns into an angel when she plays," he said. "Now, let's listen, Gratian, and afterwards you can tell me what pictures the music makes to you, and I'll tell you what it makes to me."

The organ was old and rather out of repair, and Andrew was not very well used to blowing. That made it, I think, all the more wonderful that the lady could bring such music out of it. It was not so fine and perfect, doubtless, as what Gratian had heard from her in church on the Sunday afternoon, but still it was beautiful enough for him to think of nothing but his delight in listening. She played several pieces — some sad and plaintive, some joyful and triumphant, and then Gratian begged her to play the last he had heard at church.

"That is a good choice for our good-night one,"

she said. "It is a favourite of Fergus's too. He calls it his good-night hymn."

Fergus did not speak — he was lying with his eyes shut, in quiet happiness, and as the last notes died away. "Don't speak yet, Gratian," he said. "you don't know what I am seeing — flocks of birds are slowly flying out of sight, the sun has set, and one hears a bell in the distance ringing very faintly; one by one the lights are going out in the cottages that I see at the foot of the hill, and the night is creeping up. That is what *I* see when mother plays the good-night. What do you see, Gratian?"

"The moor, I think," said the boy, "our own moor, up, far up, behind our house. It must be looking just as I see it now, at this very minute; only the music is coming from some place — a church, I think, *very* far away. The wind is bringing it — the south wind, not the one from the sea. And you know that when the music is being played in the church there are lots of people all kneeling so that you can't see their faces, and I think some are crying softly."

"Yes," said Fergus, "that isn't so bad. I can see it too. You'll soon get into the way, Gratian," he went on, with his funny little patronising tone, "of making music-pictures if we practice it together. That's the best of music, you see. It makes itself and pictures too. Now pictures never make you music."

"But they give you feelings — like telling you stories — at least that one I like so much does. And I suppose there are many pictures like that — as beautiful as that?" he went on, as if asking the question from the lady, who had left the organ now and was standing by Fergus, listening to what they were saying.

"Yes," she said, "there are many pictures I should like you to see, and many places too. Places which make one wish one could paint them the moment one sees them. Perhaps it is pictures you are going to care most for, little Gratian? If so, they will be music and poetry and everything to you — they will be your voice."

"*Poetry*," repeated Fergus, "that's the other thing — the thing I couldn't remember the name of, Gratian."

Gratian looked rather puzzled.

"I don't know much about poetry," he said. "But I don't know about anything. I never saw pictures before. There are so many things to know about," he added with a little sigh.

"Don't be discouraged," said the lady smiling. "Everybody has to find out and to learn and to work hard."

"Has everybody a voice?" asked Gratian.

"No, a great many haven't, and some who have don't use it well, which is worse than having none. But don't look so grave; we shall have plenty of time for talking about all these things. I think you must be going home now, otherwise your mother will be wondering what has become of you. And thank her for letting us have you, and say I hope you may come again on Saturday. You don't mind the long walk home — for it is almost dark, you see?"

"Oh no, I don't mind the dark or anything like that," said Gratian with a little smile, which the lady, even though her forget-me-not eyes were so very clear, could not quite understand.

For he was thinking to himself, "How could I be afraid, with my four godmothers to take care of me, wherever I were?"

Then he turned to say good-bye to Fergus, and the little fellow stretched up his two thin arms and clasped them round the moorland child's neck.

"I love you," he said: "kiss me and come again soon, and let us make stories to tell each other."

The lady kissed him too.

"Thank you for being so good to Fergus," she said.

And Gratian, looking up in her face, wished he could tell her how much he had liked all he had seen and heard, but somehow the words would not come. All he could say was, "Thank you, and good-night."

Out-of-doors again, especially when he got as far as the well-known road he passed along every day, it seemed all like a dream. All the way down the avenue of pines he kept glancing back to see the lights in the windows of the Big House — he liked

to think of Fergus and his mother in there by the
fire, talking of the afternoon and making, perhaps,
plans for another.

"I hope his back won't hurt him to-night when
they carry him up to bed," he said to himself. "It
was very good of Golden-wings to come. But I'm
afraid she can't be here much more, now that the
winter is so near. Green-wings might perhaps come
sometimes, but—"

A sudden puff of wind in his face, and a voice in
his ear, interrupted him. The wind felt sharp and
cold, and he did not need the tingling of his cheeks
to tell him who was at hand.

"But what?" said the cutting tones of Gray-wings.
"Ah, I know what you were going to say, Master
Gratian. White-wings and I are too sharp and
outspoken for your new friends! Much you know
about it. On the contrary, nothing would do the
lame boy more good than a nice blast from the north,
once he is able to be up and about again. It was
for the moorland air the doctors, with some sense for
once, sent him up here. And I am sure you must
know it isn't Golden-wings and Green-wings only
who are to be met with on the moors."

"I'm very sorry if I've offended you," said Gratian,
"but you needn't be quite so cross about it. I don't
mind you being sharp when I deserve it, but I've
been quite good to-day, *quite* good. I'm sure the
lady wouldn't like me if I wasn't good."

"Humph!" said Gray-wings. At least she meant it to be "humph," and Gratian understood it so, but to any one else it would have sounded more like "whri—i—zz," and you would have put up your hand to your head at once to be sure that your cap or hat wasn't going to fly off. "Humph! *I* don't set up to be perfect, though I might boast a little more experience, a few billions of years more, of this queer world of yours than you. And I've been pretty well snubbed in my time and kept in my proper place — to such an extent, indeed, that I don't now even quarrel with having a *very* much worse name than I deserve. It's good for one's pride, so I make a wry face and swallow it, though of course, all the same, it must be a very pleasant feeling to know that one has been quite, *quite* good. I wish you'd tell me what it's like."

"You're very horrid and unkind, Gray-wings," said Gratian, feeling almost ready to cry. "Just when I was so happy, to try and spoil it all. Tell me what you think I've not been good about and I'll listen, but you needn't go mocking at me for nothing."

There was no answer, and Gratian thought perhaps Gray-wings was feeling ashamed of herself. But he was much mistaken. She was only reserving her breath for a burst of laughter. Gratian of course knew it was laughter, though I don't suppose either you or I would have known it for that.

" What is it that amuses you so ? " asked the boy.

" It's Green-wings — you can't see her unfortu-
nately — she's posting down in such a hurry. She
thinks I tease you, and she knows I'm in rather a
mischievous mood to-night. But they've caught her
— she can't get past the corner over there, where the
Wildridge hills are — and she is in such a fuss. The
hills never like her to run past without paying them
a visit if they can help it, and she's too soft-hearted
to go on her way will-ye, nill-ye, as I do. So you'll
have to trust to me to take you home after all, my
dear godchild."

" Dear Green-wings," said Gratian, " I don't like
her to be anxious about me."

" Bless you, she's always in a pathetic humour
about some one or something," said Gray-wings.

" I don't mind you taking me home if you won't
mock at me," said Gratian. " Are you really displeased with me ? Have I done anything naughty
without knowing it ? "

Gray-wings's tone suddenly changed. Never had
her voice sounded so gentle and yet earnest.

" No, my child. I only meant to warn you. It
is my part both to correct and to warn — of the two
I would rather, by far, warn. Don't get your little
head turned — don't think there is nothing worth,
nothing beautiful, except in the new things you may
see and hear and learn. And never think yourself
quite anything. That is always a mistake. What

will seem new to you is only another way of putting the old — and the path to any real good is always the same — never think to get on faster from leaving it. You can't understand all this yet, but you will in time. Now put your arms out, darling — I am here beside you. Clasp them round my neck; never mind if it feels cold — there. I have you safe, and here goes — "

A whirl, a rapid upbearing, a rush of cold, fresh air, and a pleasant, dreamy feeling, as when one is rocked in a little boat at sea. Gratian closed his eyes — he *was* tired, poor little chap, for nothing is more tiring than new sights and feelings — and knew no more till he found himself lying on the heather, a few yards from the Farm gates.

He looked about him — it was quite night by now — he felt drowsy still, but no longer tired, and not cold — just pleasantly warm and comfortable.

"Gray-wings must have wrapped me up somehow," he said to himself. "She's very kind, really. But I must run in — what would mother think if she saw me lying here?"

And he jumped up and ran home.

The gate was open, the door of the house was open too, and just within the porch stood his mother.

"Is that you, Gratian?" she said, as she heard his step.

"Yes, mother," he replied: and as he came into the light he looked up at her. She was much, much

older-looking than Fergus's mother, for she had not
married young, and Gratian was the youngest of
several, the others of whom had died. But as he
glanced at her sunburnt face, and saw the love shining out of her eyes, tired and rather worn by daily
work as she was, she somehow reminded him of the
graceful lady with the sweet blue eyes.

"I understand some of what Gray-wings said," he
thought. "It's the same in mother's face and in hers
when she looks at Fergus."

And he held up his mouth for a kiss.

"Have you been happy at the Big House?" Mrs.
Conyfer asked. "Were they kind to you? She seems
a kind lady, if one can trust to pretty looks."

"Oh! she's very kind," answered Gratian eagerly;
"and so's Fergus. He's her boy, mother — he can't
walk, nor scarcely stand. But he's getting better —
the air here will make him better."

"It's to be hoped so, I'm sure," said the farmer's
wife, with great sympathy in her tone. "It must be
a terrible grief — the poor child — I couldn't find it in
my heart to refuse to let you go when Mr. Cornelius
told me of his affliction. But you were happy, and
they were good to you?"

"Oh, mother! yes — happier than ever I was in
my life."

Mrs. Conyfer smiled and yet sighed a little. She
knew her child was not altogether like his compeers
of the moor country — she was proud of it, and yet
sometimes afraid with a vague misgiving.

"Come in and warm yourself — it's a cold evening. There's some hot gridle cakes and a cup of Fernflower's milk for your supper — though maybe you had so many fine things to eat at the Big House that you won't be hungry."

"Ah, but I am, though," he said brightly ; and the big kitchen looked so cheery, and the little supper so tempting, that Gratian smiled with satisfaction.

"How good of you to make it so nice for me, mother!" he said. "I could never like *anywhere* better than my own home, however beautiful it was."

CHAPTER X.

THE STORY OF THE SEA-GULL.

THE FORSAKEN MERMAN.

THE winter — the real winter, such as it is known up in that country — came on slowly that year. There was no snow and but little frost before Christmas. Fergus gained ground steadily, and his mother, who at first had dreaded the experiment of the bleak but bracing air, was so encouraged that she stayed on from week to week. And through these weeks there was never a half-holiday which the two boys did not spend together.

Gratian was learning much — more than even those who knew him best had full understanding of; much, much more than he himself knew.

"He is like a different child," said the school-master one day to the lady, when she had looked in as she was passing through the village; "if you had seen him a year ago: he seemed always dreaming or

115

in the clouds. I really thought I should never succeed in teaching him anything. You have opened his mind."

"His mind had begun to open before he ever saw me, Mr. Cornelius," said Fergus's mother with a smile. "It is like a flower — it asks nothing but to be allowed to grow. He is a very uncommon child — one could imagine that some specially happy influences surrounded him. He seems to take in and to feel interest in so many different things. I wonder what he will grow up."

"Ah yes, ma'am," said the schoolmaster with a sigh. "It is a pity to think of his being no more than his father before him. But yet, what can one do?"

"One would like at least to find out what he *might* be," she said thoughtfully. "He will be a *good* man, whether he ever leaves the moors or not — of that I feel sure. And if it is his duty to stay in this quiet corner of the world, I suppose we must not regret it."

"I suppose not. I *try* to think so," said the schoolmaster. But from something in his tone the lady suspected that he was looking back rather sadly on dreams, long ago past, of his own future — dreams which had never come to pass, and left him but the village schoolmaster.

And her sympathy with this half-understood disappointment made her think still more of Gratian.

"Cornelius would live again in this child if he should turn out one of the great few," she thought to herself.

It was one of the afternoons Gratian now always spent with Fergus. She could leave her lame boy with perfect comfort in his friend's care, sure that he would be both safe and happy. As she made her way up the pine avenue and drew near to the house, she heard bright voices welcoming her.

"Mother dear," Fergus called out, "I have walked twelve times along the south terrace — six times up and six times down — with Gratian's arm. It is so sheltered there — just a nice little soft breeze. Do you know, Gratian, I so often notice that breeze when you are here? It is as if it came with you."

"But it is getting colder now, my boy," she answered. "You must come in. I have been to see Mr. Cornelius, Gratian. I am so glad to hear that he is pleased with your lessons. I would not like him to think that being with us distracted your attention."

"I'm sure it doesn't, ma'am," said Gratian simply. "So often the things you tell me about or read to us, or that I hear about somehow when I am here, seem to come in just at the right minute, and to make my lessons easier. I have never found lessons so nice as this winter."

"I don't like lessons," said Fergus. "I never shall like them."

"You will have to look upon them as necessary evils then," said his mother.

"I usen't to like them," said Gratian. "*Now* I often think I'd like to go on till I'm quite big."

"Well, so you can, can't you?" said Fergus.

"No," Gratian replied: "boys like me have to stop when they're big enough to help their fathers at home, and I've no big brother like Tony. I'll have to stop going to school before very long. I used to think I'd be very glad. Now I'd be sorry even if I was to be a shepherd."

"How do you mean?" asked the lady.

Gratian looked up at her with his soft brown eyes.

"I used to think being a shepherd and lying out on the heather all day—alone with the sheep and Watch, like old Jonas—would be the best life of any. But now I want to know things. I think one can fancy better when one knows more. And I'd like to do more than fancy."

"What would you like to do?" asked Fergus's mother. "Would you like to learn to *make* music as well as to play it? That is what Fergus wants to do."

Gratian shook his head.

"I don't know," he replied. "I don't know *yet*. And isn't it best not to plan about it, because I know father will need me on the farm?"

"Perhaps it is best," she said. But she answered as if thinking of something else at the same time.

And then Andrew came out to help Fergus up the steps into the house, where tea was waiting for them in the library.

Fergus's mother was rather tired. She had walked some distance to see a poor woman who was ill that afternoon.

"Don't ask me to play much to-day, my dear boys," she said. "I never like to play much when I am tired; it doesn't seem fair to the music."

"Then you shan't play at all, mother darling," said Fergus. "Gratian, I'll tell you what; you shall tell mother and me a story. That will rest her nicely."

Gratian looked up hesitatingly.

"He tells such nice stories," Fergus went on.

"Does he often tell them?" asked the lady.

"Yes, when we are alone," said Fergus.

"The music makes me think of them very often," said Gratian. "It makes Fergus see pictures, and it makes me think stories. Sometimes I can see pictures too, but I think I like stories best."

"He made a beauty the other day, about a Princess whose eyes were forget-me-nots, so that whoever had once seen her could never forget her again; and if they were good people it made them very happy, but if they were naughty people it made them very unhappy — only it did them all good somehow in the end. Gratian made it come right."

"That sounds very pretty," said the lady. "Did that come out of my music?"

"No," said the boy, "that story came mostly out of your eyes. I called you the lady with the forget-me-not eyes the first Sunday in church."

He spoke so simply that the lady could not help smiling.

"My eyes thank you for your pretty thoughts of them," she said. "Will you tell that story again?"

"No," Fergus interrupted. "I want a new one. You were to have one ready for to-day, Gratian."

"I have only a very little one, but I will tell it, if you like," said Gratian. "It isn't exactly like a story. There isn't anything wonderful in it like in the one about the Princess, or the one about the underground fairies."

"No, that *was* a beauty," said Fergus. "But never mind if this one isn't quite so nice," he added condescendingly.

So Gratian began.

"It is about a sea-gull," he said. "You know about them, of course, for you have been at the sea. This was a little, young sea-gull. It had not long learnt to fly, and sea-gulls need to fly very well, for often they have to go many miles without a rest when they are out at sea, unless there happens to be a ship passing or a rock standing up above the water, or even a bunch of seaweed floating — that might do for a young bird that is not very heavy. There was very stormy weather the year this sea-gull and his brothers and sisters were hatched, and sometimes the

father and mother sea-gulls were quite frightened to
let them try to fly, for fear they should be beaten
down by the storm winds and not have strength to
rise again. It is quite different, you see, from little
land-birds learning to fly. They can just flutter a
little way from one twig to another near the ground.
so that if they do fall they can't be much hurt. Sea-
gulls need to have brave hearts even when they are
quite little. This sea-gull was very brave, almost
too brave. He loved the sea so dearly that while he
was still a nestling, peeping out from his home, high
up on a ledge of rock, at the dancing, flashing waves
down below, he longed to be among them. He felt
as if he almost would go mad with joy if only his
mother would let him dash off with her, whirling and
curving about in the air, with nothing below but the
great ocean. And he would scarcely believe her and
his father when they told him that it wasn't so easy
to fly as it looked — not at the beginning, and that
birds had to learn by degrees. At last one day the
father, who had been out sniffing about, came in and
told the mother it would be a good day for a beginning. So all the four young ones got ready, and
stood at the edge of the nest in great excitement. I
think it must have been very funny to see them at
first — they were so awkward and clumsy. But they
didn't hurt themselves — for the old birds kept them
at first among the rocks where they couldn't fall far.
And our sea-gull wasn't quite so sure of himself the

next day, nor quite so impatient to go on flying, and I dare say he got on better when he had become less conceited. When they could fly a little better the father and mother took them to a little bay, where there was nice soft sand, and where the wind blew gently, and there they got on very well. And there they should have been content to stay till the spring storms were over and their wings had grown stronger. They were all quite content except the one I am telling you of."

"What was his name?" asked Fergus.

"He hasn't got one," Gratian replied, "but we can make him one. I dare say it would be better."

"Call him White-wings," said Fergus.

"No," said Gratian, "that won't do," though he didn't say why. "Besides his wings weren't all white. We'll call him 'Quiver,' because he was always quivering with impatience. Well, they were all quite content except Quiver, and he was very discontented. He looked longingly over the sea, wishing so to be in the midst of the flocks of birds he saw sparkling in the sunshine; and at last one morning when his father and mother had gone off for a good fly for themselves, which they well deserved, poor things, after all there trouble with the little ones, he stood up in the nest, flapping his impatient wings, and said to the three others that he too was going off on his own account. The brothers and sisters begged him not, but it was no use — off he would go, he was in such a hurry to see the world and to feel independent. Well, he got on pretty well at first; the sea was far out, and there were several rocks sticking up which he could rest on, and he found it so easy that he was tempted to fly out farther than he had intended. going from one rock to the other. And he didn't notice how far he had gone till he had been resting a while on a rock a good way out, and then looking round he couldn't tell a bit where he was, for there was nothing but sea all round him. He couldn't think what had become of all the other points of rocks — they seemed to have disappeared. But just as he was beginning to feel rather frightened a number of gulls flew up and lighted on the rock. They were all chattering and very excited.

"'We must make haste,' they said, 'and get to the shore as fast as we can before the storm is on us. And we must shelter there till we can get back to our own rocks.'

"They only rested a moment or two, and then got ready to start again. Quiver stood up and flapped his wings to attract attention.

"'May I fly with you?' he said. 'I'm afraid I don't quite know the way.'

"They looked at him in surprise.

"'What are you doing away from your home — a young fledgling like you?' they said. 'Come with us if you like, it's your only chance, but you'll probably never get to shore.'

"Oh how frightened he was, and how he wished he'd stayed at home! But he flew away with them, for it was, as they said, his only chance, and what he suffered was something dreadful. And when at last he reached the shore, it was only to drop down and lie on the sands gasping and bruised, and, as he thought, dying. A man that was passing, in a hurry himself to get home before the storm, picked up poor Quiver, half out of pity, half because he thought his little master might like to have his feathers if he died, or to make a pet of him if he lived. And Quiver, who was quite fainting by this time, woke up to find himself lying in a little sort of tool-house in a garden, with a boy about as big as you, Fergus, stooping over him.

"'I don't think he's going to die,' the boy said. 'I've made him a bed of some hay here in the corner — to-morrow we'll see how he is.'

"Poor Quiver felt very strange and queer and sad. It took him several days to get better, and he didn't like the food they gave him, though of course they meant to be kind. At last, one day he was able to hop about and even to flap his wings a little.

"'Now I shall soon be able to fly home again,' he thought joyfully. 'If once I can get to the sea I'll be sure to meet some gulls who can show me the way.'

"And when the boy came to look at him, he was pleased to hear himself said to be quite well again.

"'We can let him out into the garden now, can't we?' he said to the gardener, 'and we'll see if he's such a good slug catcher as you say.'

"'No fear but he's that, sir.' said the gardener. 'But first we must clip his wings, else he'd be flying away.'

"And he took Quiver up in his arms, and stretching out his wings, though not so as to hurt them, snipped at them with a big sharp pair of scissors. Quiver didn't feel it, any more than we feel having our nails cut, but he was dreadfully frightened. And he was still all shaking and confused when the gardener set him down on the garden path—though he got better in a minute and looked about him. It was a pretty garden, and he was pleased to be out in the air again, though he felt something strange in it, for he had never before been away from the sea. And he ran a few steps just to try his legs, and then turned round meaning to say good-bye to the boy and thank him in his sea-gull way for his hospitality before starting off. Having done this he stretched his wings to fly — but — oh dear, what was the matter? He could not raise himself more than a few inches from the ground — wings!—he had none left, and with a pitiful cry he rolled over on the ground in misery and despair.

"'Poor bird!' said the boy; 'you shouldn't have clipped his wings, Barnes. It would have been better to let him fly away.'

"'He'd never have got to his home; he's too young a bird to fly so far. And he'll be uncommon good for the slugs, you'll see, sir.'

"So all the summer poor Quiver spent in the garden. He got more used to it after a while, but still he had always a pain at his heart. He used to rush along the paths as if he was in a desperate hurry and eager to get to the end, and then he would just rush back again. It was the only way he could keep down his impatience and his longing for the sea. He used to pretend to himself that when he got to the end of the path he would feel the salt air and see the waves dancing; but the children of the house, who of course didn't understand his thoughts, used to laugh at him and call him 'that absurd creature.' But his heart was too sore for him to mind, and even catching slugs was very little consolation to him.

" And so Quiver lived all through the summer and the autumn till the winter came round again, and all this time whenever his wings began to grow longer, Barnes snipped them short again. I don't think there ever was a bird so severely punished for discontent and impatience.

" The winter was a dreadfully cold one; there was frost for such a long time that nothing seemed alive at all — there was not a worm or a slug or an insect of any kind in the garden. The little boy and his brothers and sisters all went away when it began to get so cold, but before they went, they told Barnes that he must not leave Quiver out in the garden; he must be shut up for the winter in the large poultry house with the cocks and hens.

" 'For there's nothing for him to eat outside, and you might forget to feed him, you know,' the children said.

" So Quiver passed the winter safely, though sadly enough. He had plenty to eat, and no one teased or ill-used him, but he used sometimes almost to *choke* with his longing for freedom and for the fresh air — above all, the air of the sea. He did not know how long winter lasted; he was still a young bird, but he often felt as if he would die if he were kept a prisoner much longer. But he had to bear it, and he didn't die, and he grew at last so patient that no one would have thought he was the same discontented bird. There was a little yard covered over with netting outside the hen-house, and Quiver could see the sky from there; and the clouds scudding along when it was a windy day reminded him a little of the waves he feared he would never see again; and the stupid, peaceful cocks and hens used to wonder what he found to stare up at for hours together. *They* thought by far the most interesting thing in life was to poke about on the ground for the corn that was thrown out to them.

" At last — at last — came the spring. It came by little bits at a time of course, and Quiver couldn't understand what made everything feel so different, and why the sky looked blue again, till one day the gardener's wife, who managed the poultry, opened the door of the covered yard and let them all out, and Quiver, being thinner and quicker than the hens, slipped past her and got out into the garden. She saw him when he had got there, but she thought it was all right — he might begin his slug-catching again. And he hurried along the path in his old way, feeling thankful to be free, but with the longing at his heart, stronger than ever. It was so long since he had tried to fly in the least that he had forgotten almost that he had wings, and he just went hurrying along on his legs. All of a sudden something startled him — a noise in the trees or something like that — and without thinking what he was doing, he stretched his wings in the old way. But fancy his surprise; instead of flopping and lopping about as they had done for so long, ever since Barnes had cut them, they stood out firm and steady, quite able to support his weight; he tried them again, and then again, and — it was no mistake — up he soared, up, up, up, into the clear spring sky, strong and free and fearless, for his wings had grown again! That was what they had been doing all the long dull winter; so happiness came to poor Quiver at last, when he had learnt to wait."

"And did he fly home?" asked Fergus breathlessly; "did he find his father and mother and the others in the old nest among the rocks?"

"Yes," replied Gratian, after a moment's consideration, "he met some gulls on his way to the sea, who told him exactly how to go. And he did find them all at home. You know, generally, bird families don't stay so long together, but these gulls had been so unhappy about Quiver that they had fixed to stay close to the old ones till he came back. They always kept on hoping he would come back."

"I am so glad," said Fergus with a sigh of relief. "How beautiful it must have been to feel the sea-wind again, and see the waves dancing in the sunshine! Do you know, Gratian, I was just a little afraid at the end that you were going to say that Quiver had grown so good that he went 'up, up, up,' straight into heaven. I shouldn't have liked that — at least not till he had lived happily by the sea first. And then," Fergus began to get a little confused, "I don't know about that. *Do* gulls go to heaven, mother? You don't mind my thinking dogs do."

The lady smiled. She had not said anything yet; she seemed to be thinking seriously. But now she drew Gratian to her and kissed his forehead.

"Thank you, dear boy," she said. "I am so glad to have heard one of your stories."

CHAPTER XI.

DRAWN TWO WAYS.

GRATIAN almost danced along the moor path on his way home that evening; he felt so happy. Never had he loved Fergus and his mother so much — he could not now understand how he had ever lived without them, and like a child he did not think of how he ever *could* do so. He let the future take care of itself.

It was cold of course. He rather fancied that White-wings was not far off, and once or twice he stood still to listen. It was some little time now since he had heard anything of his friends. But at first nothing met his ear, and he ran on.

Suddenly a breath — a waft rather of soft air blew over his face. It was not White-wings, and most certainly not Gray-wings. Gratian looked up in surprise — he could hardly expect the soft western sister on such a cold night.

"Yes, it is I," she said; "you can hardly believe it, can you? I am only passing by — no one else will know I have been here. I don't generally come

when you are in such merry spirits — I don't feel
that you need me then. But as I was not so very
far off, I thought I'd give you a kiss on my way.
So you told them the sea-gull's story — I am glad
they liked it."

"Yes," said Gratian, "they did. indeed. But,
Green-wings, I'm glad you've come, for I wanted to
ask you, if they asked me if I made it all up myself,
what can I say? I'm so afraid of telling what isn't
true; but you know I couldn't explain about you
and the others. I couldn't if I tried."

"You are not meant to do so," replied she quickly.
"What have you said when Fergus has asked you
about other stories?"

"I have said I couldn't explain how I knew them
— that sometimes they were a sort of dream. I
didn't want to say I had made them all myself,
though I have *partly* made them — you know I have,
Green-wings."

"Certainly — it was not I for instance, who told
you the very remarkable fact of natural history that
you related at the end of the story?" said Green-
wings with her soft laugh. "You may quite take
the credit of that. But I won't laugh at you, dear.
It is true that they are your stories, and yet a sort of
dream. No one but you could hear them — no one
would say that the whispers of the wind talking
language to you, are anything but the reflection of
your own pretty fancies. It will be all right — you

will see. But I must go," and she gave a little sigh.

"Green-wings, darling, you seem a little sad to-night," said Gratian. "Why is it? Is it that the winter has come?"

"I am never very merry. as you know. But I am a little sadder than usual to-night. I foresee — I foresee sorrows"—and her voice breathed out the words with such an exquisite plaintiveness that they sounded like the dying away notes of a dirge. "But keep up your heart, my darling, and trust us all — all four. We only wish your good, though we may show it in different ways. And wherever I am I can always be with you to comfort you, if it be but for a moment. No distance can separate us from our child."

"And I am most *your* child, am I not, dear Green-wings?" asked Gratian. "I knew you the first, and I think I love you the most."

"My darling, good-night," whispered Green-wings, and with a soft flutter she was gone.

There was no mother waiting at the open door for Gratian's return that evening.

"It is too cold for standing outside now," he said to himself as he went in, adding aloud, "Here I am. mother. Did you think I was late?"

Mrs. Conyfer was sitting by the fire. Her knitting lay on her knee, but her hands were idle. She looked up as Gratian came in.

"ARE YOU NOT WELL, MOTHER?" HE SAID GENTLY.—p. 133.

"I am glad you have come, dear," she said; but her voice sounded tired, and when he was close to her he saw that her face seemed tired also.

"Are you not well, mother?" he said gently.

Mrs. Conyfer looked a little surprised but pleased too. It was new to her either to think of how she was or to be asked about it. For though her husband was kind and good, he was plain and even a little rough, as are the moorland people in general. Gratian had never been rough, but he had not had the habit of much noticing those about him. Since he had been so often with Fergus and the lady he had learnt to be more observant of others, especially of his mother, and more tender in his manner.

"Are you not well, mother dear?" he repeated.

"I'm only a bit tired, my boy," she said. "I'm getting old, I suppose, and I've worked pretty hard in my way — not to say as if I'd been a poor man's wife of course, but a farmer's wife has a deal on her mind."

"And you do everything so well, mother," said Gratian admiringly. "I'm getting old enough now to see how different things are here from what they are in many houses. Fergus does so like to hear about the dairy and the cocks and hens, and about the girdle cakes and all the nice things you make."

"He's really a nice little gentleman!" said Mrs. Conyfer, well pleased. "I *am* glad to hear he's getting so much better. I'm sure his mother deserves he should — such a sweet lady as she is."

For now and then on a Sunday the two boys' mothers had spoken to each other.

"Yes, he's *much* better," said Gratian. "To-day he walked six times up and down the terrace with only my arm."

"They weren't afraid to let him out, and it so cold to-day?" said Mrs. Conyfer.

"It wasn't so very cold — you usedn't to mind the cold, mother," said the boy.

"Maybe not so much as now," she replied. "I think I'm getting rheumatic like my father and mother before me, for I can't move about so quick, and then one feels the cold more."

"What makes people have rheumatics?" asked Gratian.

"Folk don't have it so much hereabout," his mother answered; "but I don't belong to the moor country, you know. My home was some way from this, down in the valley, where it's milder but much damper — and damp is worst of anything for rheumatism. Dear me, I remember my old grandmother a perfect sight with it — all doubled up — you wondered how she got about. But she was a marvel of patience, and so cheery too. I only hope I shall be like her in that, if I live so long, for it's a sore trial to an active nature to become so nearly helpless."

"Had she nobody to be kind to her when she got so ill?" asked Gratian.

"Oh yes; her children were all good to her, so far as they could be. But they were all married and about in the world, and busy with their own families. She was a good deal alone, poor old grandmother."

"Mother," said Gratian quickly. "If you ever got to be like that, I would never marry or go about in the world. I'd stay at home to be a comfort to you. I'd run all your messages and do everything I could for you. Mother, I wish you'd let me be more use to you now already, even though you're not so ill."

Mrs. Conyfer smiled, but there was more pleasure than amusement in her smile.

" I do think being at the Big House has done you good, Gratian. You never used to notice or think of things so much before you went there," she said. " And you're getting very handy, there's no doubt. I hope I shall never be so laid aside, but I'm sure you'd do your best, my dear. Now I think I shall go to bed, and you must be off too. Father's out still — he and Jonas have so much to see to these cold nights, seeing that all the creatures are warm and sheltered. There's snow not far off, they were saying. The wind's in the north."

Gratian's dreams were very grotesque that night. He dreamt that his mother was turned into a sea-gull, all except her face, which remained the same. And she could neither walk nor fly, she was so lame and stiff, or else it was that her wings were cut — he was not sure which. Then he heard Green-wings's voice saying, "She only wants a sight of the sea to make her well. Gratian, you should take her to the sea; call the cocks and hens to help you;" and with that he thought he opened his eyes and found himself on the terrace where he had been walking with Fergus, and there was a beautiful little carriage drawn by about a dozen cocks and hens; but when he would have got in, Fergus seemed to push him back, saying, "Not yet, not yet, your mother first," and Fergus kept looking for Mrs. Conyfer as if he did not know that she was the poor sea-gull, standing there looking very funny with the little red knitted shawl on that Gratian's mother wore when it was a chilly morning. And just then there came flying down from above, Gratian's four friends. Nobody seemed to see them but himself, and the cocks and hens began making such a noise that he felt quite confused.

"Oh, do take poor mother," he called out — for there was no use trying to make any one else understand — "Green-wings and all of you, do take poor mother."

"Not without you, Gratian," replied Gray-wings's sharp voice. "It's your place to look after your mother," and as she spoke she stooped towards him and he felt her cold breath, and with the start it gave him he awoke.

The door of his room had blown open, and the window was rattling, and the clothes had slipped off on one side. No wonder he had dreamt he was cold. He covered himself up again and went to sleep.

Mrs. Conyfer was up as usual the next morning. She said she was better, but she limped a little as she walked, and Gratian did not like to see it, though she assured him it did not hurt her.

"I shall take a rest on Sunday," she said, "and then you may tend me a bit, Gratian. He's as handy as a girl," she added, turning to the farmer with a smile. And Mr. Conyfer patted his son's head.

"That's right," he said; "always be good to your mother."

"Winter is really coming," thought Gratian, as he ran to school, and he glanced up at the sky wondering if snow were at last on the way.

It held off however for some little time yet.

It was on the third day after this that Gratian on his way home was rather surprised to meet Mr. Cornelius returning as if from the Farm. The school-children knew that the master had been somewhere, for he had left the school in charge of one or two of the head boys and his sister, who lived with him and taught the girls sewing.

He smiled and nodded at Gratian, but did not speak, and the boy could not help wondering if he had been at Four Winds, and why. And as soon as he got home he ran eagerly in to ask.

"Has the master been here, mother? What did he come for?" he called out.

His father and mother were both together in the kitchen, talking rather earnestly.

His father looked at him as he answered —

"Yes, Gratian," he said, "Mr. Cornelius has been here. He had something important to talk to us about. After you have had your tea and done your lessons we will tell you."

"I haven't any lessons, father," he replied. "We had time to do them this afternoon when the master was out."

So as soon as tea was over he was told what it was.

"Your friends at the Big House," began the farmer, "are leaving soon. They daren't stay once it gets really cold. You'll be sorry to lose them, my boy?"

Gratian felt a lump rise in his throat, but he tried to answer cheerfully.

"Yes, father. They've been so good to me. I knew they'd have to go sometime, but I tried not to think of it. The lady has taught me so many things I never knew before. I'll try not to forget them."

"She has been very good to you, and she wants to be still more. That's what Cornelius came about. I don't want to make you vain, Gratian, but she thinks, and Cornelius thinks — and they should know — that there's the making of something out of the common in you — that, if you are taught and trained the right way, you may come to be something a good bit higher than a plain moorland farmer."

Gratian listened with wide-opened eyes.

"I know," he said breathlessly, "I've felt it sometimes. I don't rightly know what. I'd like to learn — I'd like to — oh, father, I can't say what I mean. It's as if there were so many thoughts in me that I can't say," and the child leaned his head on his mother's shoulder and burst into tears.

The farmer and his wife looked at each other. They were simple unlettered folk, but for all that there was something in them that "understood."

"My boy, my little Gratian," said the mother, in tones that she but seldom used; "don't cry, my dear. Listen to father."

And in a moment or two the child raised his still tearful eyes, and the farmer went on.

"It's just that," he said. "It's just because you can't rightly say, that we want you to learn. No one can tell as yet what your talent may be, or if perhaps it is not, so to speak, but an everyday one after all. If so, no harm will be done; for you will be in wise hands, and you will come home again to Four Winds and follow in your father's and grandfather's steps. But your friends think you should have a better chance of learning and seeing for yourself than I can give you here. And the lady has written to her husband, and he's quite willing, and so it's, so to speak, all settled. You are to go with them when they leave here, Gratian, and for a year or so you are to have lessons at home with the little boy, who isn't yet strong enough to go to school. And by the end of that time it'll be easier to see what you are best fitted for. You'll have teaching of all kinds — music and drawing, and all sorts of book-learning. It's a handsome offer, there's no denying."

And the tears quite disappeared from Gratian's bright eyes, and his whole face glowed with hope and satisfaction.

"I'll do my best, father. I can promise you that. You shall have no call to be ashamed of me. It's very good of you and mother to let me go. But I shall come home again before very long — I shan't be long without seeing you?"

"Oh yes — you shall come home after a while of course. Anyway for a visit, and to see how it will be best to do. We're not going to give you away altogether, you may be sure," said the farmer with a little attempt at a joke.

But the mother did not speak. She kissed the boy as she rarely kissed him, and whispered "God bless you, my dear," when she bade him good-night.

"I wonder if it's all come of our giving him such an outlandish name!" said Mrs. Conyfer with a rather melancholy smile.

And Gratian fell asleep with his mind in a whirl.

"I should like to talk about it to my godmothers," was almost his last thought. "I wonder if I shall still see them sometimes when I am far from Four Winds."

And the next morning when he woke, he lay looking round his little room and thinking how much he liked it, and how happy he had been in it. He was beginning to realise that no good is all good, no light without shadow.

But there seemed no shadow or drawback of any kind the next day when he went to the Big House to talk it all over with the lady and Fergus. Fergus was too delighted for words.

"It is like a story in a book, isn't it, Gratian?" he said. "And if you turn out a great man, then the world will thank mother and me for having found you."

Gratian blushed a little.

"I don't know about being a *great* man," he said, "but I want to find out really what it is I can do best, and then it will be my own fault if I don't do *something* good."

"Yes, my boy — that is exactly what I want you to feel," said Fergus's mother.

But Gratian was anxious to know what his four friends had to say about it.

"I don't think it's very kind of none of you to come to speak to me," he said aloud on his way home. "I know you're not far off—all of you. I'm sure I heard Gray-wings scolding outside last night."

A sound of faint laughter up above him seemed to answer.

"Oh there you are, Gray-wings, I thought as much," he said, buttoning up his jacket, for it was very cold. But he had hardly spoken before he heard, nearer than the laughter had been, a soft sigh.

"I never forget you—remember, Gratian, whenever you want me—whenever in sor—row."

"That's Green-wings," he said to himself. "But why should she talk of sorrow when I'm so happy— happier than ever in my life, I think. She *is* of rather too melancholy a nature."

He ran on—the door was latched—he hurried into the kitchen. There was no one there.

"Where can mother be?" he thought. He heard steps moving upstairs and turned to go there. Half-way up he met Madge, the servant, coming down. Her face looked anxious and distressed through all its rosiness.

"Oh the poor missis," she said. "She's had to go to bed. The pains in her ankles and knees got so bad—I'm afeared she's going to be really very ill."

Gratian ran past her into his mother's room.

"Don't be frightened," Mrs. Conyfer said at once. "It's only that my rheumatism is very bad to-day. I'll be better in the morning, dear. I must be well with you going away so soon."

And when the farmer came in she met him with the same cheerful tone, though it was evident she was suffering severely.

But Gratian sat by her bedside all the evening, doing all he could. He was grave and silent, for the thought was deep in his heart —

"I can't go away — I can't and I mustn't if mother is going to be really ill. Poor mother! I'm sure my godmothers wouldn't think I should."

CHAPTER XII.

"If all the beauty in the earth
And skies and hearts of men
Were gently gathered at its birth,
And loved and born again."

MATTHEW BROWNE.

BUT the godmothers seemed to have forgotten him. He went sadly to bed — and the tears came to his eyes when he remembered how that very evening he had thought of himself as "happier than he had ever been in his life." He fell asleep however as one does at nine years old, whatever troubles one has, and slept soundly for some hours. Then he was awakened by his door opening and some one coming in. It was his father.

"Gratian, wake up. Your mother is very ill I'm afraid. Some one must go for the doctor — old Jonas is the nearest. I can't leave her — she seems nearly unconscious. Dress yourself as quick as you can, and tell Jonas to bring Dr. Spense as soon as possible."

Gratian was up and dressed almost at once. He felt giddy and miserable, and yet with a strange feeling over him that he had known it all before.

He dared not try to think clearly — he dared not face the terrible fear at the bottom of his heart. It was his first experience of real trouble.

As he hurried off he met Madge at the door: she too had been wakened up. A sudden thought struck him.

"Madge," he said, "if I'm not back quickly, tell father not to be frightened. I think I'll go all the way for the doctor myself. It'll save time not to go waking old Jonas, and I know he couldn't go as fast as I can."

Madge looked admiringly and yet half-anxiously at the boy. He seemed such a little fellow to go all that way alone in the dark winter night.

"I dare say you're right," she said. "and yet I'm half-afraid. Hadn't you better ask master first?"

Gratian shook his head.

"No, no. It will be all right. Don't trouble him about me unless he asks," and off he ran.

He went as quickly as he could find his way — it was not a *very* dark night — till he was fairly out on the moorland path. Then he stood still.

"White-wings, Green-wings — whichever of you hears me, come and help me. Dear Green-wings, you said you always would comfort me."

"So she would, surely," said a voice, firmer and colder than hers, but kindly too, "but at this moment it's more strength than comfort that you want. Hold out your arms, my boy, there — clasp me tight, don't start at my cold breath. That's right. Why, I can fly with you as if you were a snow-flake!"

And again Gratian felt the strange, whirling, rushing sensation, again he closed his eyes as if he were falling asleep, and knew no more till he found himself standing in the village street, a few doors from the doctor's house, and felt, rather than heard, a clear cold whisper of "Farewell, Gratian, for the present."

And the next morning the neighbours spoke of the sudden northern blast that had come rushing down from the moors in the night, and wondered it had not brought the snow with it, little thinking it had brought a little boy instead!

Dr. Spense was soon awakened, and long as the time always seems to an anxious watcher by a sick-bed, Farmer Conyfer could scarcely believe his ears when he heard the rattle of the dogcart wheels up the steep road, or his eyes when the doctor, followed by Gratian, came up the staircase.

"My boy, but you have done bravely!" said the father in amazement. "Doctor, I can't understand how he can have been so quick!"

The doctor turned kindly to Gratian.

"Go down, my good child, and warm yourself. I saw the sparkle of a nice fire in the kitchen — it is a bitter night. I will keep my promise to you; as I go away I'll look in."

For Gratian, though not able to tell much of his

mother's illness, had begged the doctor to promise to tell him the truth as to what he thought of her.

"I'd rather know, sir, I would indeed, even if it's very bad," he had said tremblingly.

And as he sat by the kitchen fire waiting, it seemed to him that never till now had he in the least understood how he loved his mother.

It was a queer, boisterous night surely. For down the chimney, well-built and well-seasoned as it was, there came a sudden swirl of wind. But strangely enough it did not make the fire smoke. And Gratian, anxious though he was, smiled as a pretty green light seemed suddenly to dance among the flames. And he was neither surprised nor startled when a soft voice whispered in his ear:

"I am here, my darling. I *would* come for one moment, though White-wings has been trying to blow me away. Keep up your heart — and don't lose hope."

And just then the doctor came in.

"My boy," he said, as he stood warming his hands at the blaze, "I will tell you the truth. I am afraid your poor mother is going to be ill for a good while. She has not taken care of herself. But I have good hopes that she will recover. And you may do a good deal. I see you are sensible, and handy, I am sure. You must be instead of a daughter to her for a while — it will be hard on your father, and you may be of great help."

Gratian thanked him, with the tears, which would not now be kept back, in his eyes. And promising to come again that same day, for it was now past midnight, the doctor went away.

Some days passed — the fever was high at first, and poor Mrs. Conyfer suffered much. But almost sooner than the doctor had ventured to hope, she began to get a little better. Within a week she was out of danger. And then came Fergus's mother again. She had already come to ask for news of her little friend's mother, and in the first great anxiety she said nothing of the plans that had been made. But now she asked to see the farmer, and talked with him some time downstairs while Gratian watched by his mother.

"I am so thankful to be better — so very thankful to be better before you go, Gratian," said the poor woman.

"Oh yes, dear mother, we cannot be thankful enough," the boy replied. "I will never forget that night — the night you were so very ill," he said with a shiver at the thought of it.

"I shall not be able to write much to you, my child," she said. "The doctor says my hands and joints will be stiff for a good while, but that I must try not to fret, and to keep an easy mind. I will try — but it won't be easy for me that's always been so stirring. And I shall miss you at first, of course. But if you're well and happy — and it would have been sad and dull for you here with me so different."

Just then the farmer's voice came sounding up the stairs.

"Gratian," it said, "come down here."

The boy obeyed. But first he stooped and kissed the pale face on the pillow.

"Dear mother," he said.

His father was standing by the kitchen fire when he went in, and the lady was seated in one of the big old arm-chairs. She looked at him with fresh love and interest in her sweet blue eyes.

"Dear Gratian," she said, "Fergus is fretting for you sadly. Your father has been telling me what a clever sick-nurse you are. And indeed I was sure of it from your way with Fergus. I am so very, very glad your dear mother is better."

"She will miss him a good deal at first. I'm afraid," said the farmer. "but I must do my best. It's about your going, my boy — the lady has already put it off some days for your sake. It's very good of you, ma'am — *very* good. I'll get him ready as well as I can. You'll excuse it if his things are not just in such shipshape order as his mother would have had them."

"Of course, of course," she replied. "Then the day after to-morrow. I *daren't* wait longer — the doctor says Fergus must not risk more cold as yet."

Gratian had listened in silence. But now he turned, first to his father and then to the lady, and spoke.

"Father, dear lady," he began, "don't be vexed with me — oh don't. But I can't go now. I've thought about it all these days — I'm — I'm *dreadfully* sorry," and here his voice faltered. "I wanted to learn and to understand. But it wouldn't be right. I know it wouldn't. Mother would not get well so quick without me, perhaps she'd never get well at all. And no learning or seeing things would do me really good if I knew I wasn't doing right. Father — tell me that you think I'm right."

The lady and the farmer looked at each other; there were tears in the lady's eyes.

"Is he right?" asked Gratian's father.

She bent her head.

"I'm afraid he is," she said, "but it is only fair to let him quite understand. It isn't merely putting it off for a while, Gratian," she went on; "I'm afraid it may be for altogether. We are not likely to come back to this part of the country again, and my husband, though kind, is a little peculiar. He has a nephew whom he will send for as a companion to Fergus if you don't come. We should like you better, but it is our duty to do something for Jack, and Fergus needs a companion, so it seems only natural to take him instead of sending him away to school."

"Of course," said the farmer, looking at his son.

"Yes, I understand," said Gratian. "But it doesn't make any difference. If I never learnt anything more — of learning, I mean — if I never left Four Winds or saw any of the beautiful places and things in the world, it *shouldn't* make any difference. I couldn't ever be happy or — or — do anything really good or great," he went on, blushing a little, "if I began by doing wrong — could I?"

"He is right," said his father and Fergus's mother together.

And so it was settled.

The person the most difficult to satisfy that he *was* right was — no, not Fergus — sorry as he was he loved his own mother too much not to agree — poor Mrs. Conyfer herself, for whom the sacrifice was to be made. Gratian had to talk to her for ever so long, to assure her that it was for his own sake as well — that he would have been too miserable about her to have got any good from his new opportunities. And in the end she gave in, and allowed herself to enjoy the comfort of her little boy's care and companionship during her long weary time of slow recovery.

Fergus and his mother did not leave a day too soon. With early January the winter spirits, chained hitherto, broke forth in fury. Never had such falls of snow been known even in that wild region, and many a night Gratian, lying awake, unable to sleep through the rattle and racket, felt a strange excitement at the thought that all this was the work of his mysterious protectors.

" White-wings and Gray-wings seem really going mad," he thought once or twice. But the sound of laughter, mingling with the whistling and roaring and shrieking in the chimney, reassured him.

" No fear, no fear," he seemed to hear; " we must let our spirits out sometimes. But you'd better not go to school for a day or two, small Gratian, all the same."

And several " days or two " that winter it was impossible for him to go to school, or for any one to come to the Farm, so heavy and dark even at mid-day were the storm-clouds, so deep lay the treacherous snow-drifts. Not even the doctor could reach them. But fortunately Mrs. Conyfer was by this time much better. All she now required was care and rest.

" Oh, mother dear, how glad I am that I did not leave you!" Gratian would often say. " How dull and dreary and long the days would have seemed! You couldn't even have got letters from me."

And the lessons he learnt in that winter of patient waiting, of quiet watching and self-forgetfulness, bore their fruit.

And his four friends did not forget him. There came now and then a soft breath from the two gentle sisters whose voices were hushed to all others for a time, and more than once in some mysterious way Gratian felt himself summoned out to the lonely moorland by the two whose carnival time it was.

And standing out there with the great sweep of open country all around him, with his hair tossed by White-wing's giant touch, or his cheeks tingling with a sharp blast from mischievous Gray-wings, Gratian laughed with pleasure and daring enjoyment.

"I am your child too — Spirits of the North and East. You can't frighten me. I defy you."

And the two laughed and shouted with wild glee at their foster-child's great spirit.

"He does us credit," they cried, though old Jonas passing by heard nothing but a shriek of fresh fury up above, and shouted to Gratian to hasten within shelter.

But winter never lasts for ever. Spring came again — slow and reluctant — and it was long before Gray-wings consented to take her yearly nap and let her sister of the west soothe and comfort the storm-tossed country. And then, as day by day Gratian made his way to school, he watched with awakened and ever-awaking eyes the exquisite eternal beauty of the summer's gradual approach, till at last Golden-wings clasped him in her arms one morning and told him her joy at being able to return.

"For I love this country, though no one will

believe it," she said. " The scent of the gorse and the heather is delicious and refreshing after the strong spice perfumes of my own home;" and many a story she told the child, and many a song she sang to him through the long summer days — which he loved to spend in his old way, out among the heather with Jonas and Watch and the browsing sheep.

For the holidays had begun. His mother was well, quite well, by now, and Gratian was free to do as he chose.

He was out on the moors one day — a lovely cloudless day, that would have been sultry anywhere else — when old Jonas startled him by saying suddenly:

" Did you know, Master Gratian, that the gentry's come back to the Big House?"

Gratian sat straight up in his astonishment.

" No, Jonas. How did you hear it?"

" Down in the village, quite sudden-like. It was all got ready for them last week, but there's been none of us down there much lately."

Gratian felt too excited to lie still and dream any more.

" I'll ask mother if I may go and see," he said jumping up. And off he ran. But an unexpected sight met him at a stone's throw from the Farm. It was Fergus, little lame Fergus, mounted on a tiny rough-coated pony, coming towards him! And the joy of the meeting who could describe?

It was Fergus, little lame Fergus, mounted on a tiny rough-coated pony, coming towards him!—p. 154.

"We tried to keep it a secret till it was quite sure," said the boy. "There was some difficulty about it, but it is all settled now. Father has taken the Big House from our cousin, and we are to live at it half the year. We are all there — my sisters — and my big brother comes sometimes — and mother of course. All except Jack. Jack has gone to sea. He was very nice, but he hated lessons — he only wanted to go to sea. So we want you now, Gratian — my own Gratian. I have a tutor, and you are to learn with me all the summer and to go away with us in the winter now your mother is well, so that you will find out what you want to be. It is for me we have come here. I must always be lame, Gratian. The doctors can't cure me," and the bright voice faltered. "But I shall get strong all the same if I live here in this beautiful air. And I shall be very happy, for I can learn to play on the organ — and that makes up for all."

And all came about as Fergus said.

The summer and the autumn that followed, Gratian studied with his friend's tutor. And the winter after, greatly to his mother's joy, he went away as had been planned before. But not for ever of course. No great length of time passed without his returning to his birthplace.

"I should die," he said sometimes, "if I could not from time to time stand at the old porch and feel the breath of the four winds about me."

This is only the story of the very opening of the life of a boy who lived to make his mark among men. How he did so, how he found his voice, it is not for me to tell. But he had early learnt to choose the right, and so we know he prospered.

Besides — was he not the godchild of the Four Winds of Heaven?

THE END.

"Are—— are you a mermaid, or a—that other thing?' asked the child."

P. 136.

THE CHILDREN
OF THE CASTLE
BY
MRS MOLESWORTH
ILLUSTRATED BY
WALTER CRANE
LONDON: 1893
MACMILLAN & CO
BEDFORD ST

SOME "FORGET-ME-NOTS"

FOR

My dear Venetia

19 SUMNER PLACE, S.W.
19th May, 1890

THE CHILDREN OF THE CASTLE.

CHAPTER I.

RUBY AND MAVIS.

Do you remember Gratian — Gratian Conyfer, the godson of the four winds, the boy who lived at the old farm-house up among the moors, where these strange beautiful sisters used to meet? Do you remember how full of fancies and stories Gratian's little head was, and how sometimes he put them into words to please Fergus, the lame child he loved so much? The story I am now going to tell you is one of these. I think it was their favourite one. I cannot say that it is in the very words in which Gratian used to tell it, for it was not till long, long after those boyish days that it came to be written down. But all the same it is his story.

How long ago it was I cannot say, nor can I tell you exactly where it was. This is not a story for

which you will require an atlas, nor a history of
England or of any other country, nor a dictionary of
dates. All those wise and clever and useful things
you may put out of your heads for a bit. I am just
going to tell you a story. It was somewhere and
somewhen, and I think that will do.

The "it" was a castle — and something else. But
first about the castle. It was really worthy of the
name, for it was very old and very strong, and in
ancient days it had been used as a place of defence,
and had a look about it of not having forgotten this.
(I am afraid this sounds a *very* little historical. I
must take care.) It was very big too, towering over
the sea-washed cliffs on which it stood as if defying
the winds and the waves to do their worst, frowning
at them with the little round window-eyes of its turrets, like a cross old ogre. But it was a two-faced
castle; it was only on one side — the rocky side,
where the cliffs went down precipitously to the
water — that it looked grim and forbidding. Inland,
you could scarcely have believed it was the same
castle at all. For here, towards the sunny south, it
seemed to change into a gracious, comfortable, hospi-
tably-inviting mansion; it did not look nearly so
high on this side, for the ivy-covered turrets had
more the effect of dimly dark trees in the background, and the bright wide-windowed rooms opened
on to trim lawns and terraces gay with flowers.
That was the case in summer-time at least. The

whole look of things varied a good deal according to
the seasons. In winter, grim as it was, I don't know
but that the fortress-front, so to speak, of the great
building had the best of it. For it was grand to
watch the waves breaking down below when you
knew you were safe and cosy behind the barred panes
of the turret windows, those windows pierced in the
walls through such a thickness of stone that each
was like a little room within a room. And even in
winter there were wonderful sunsets to be seen from
the children's favourite turret-room — the one which
had two windows to the west and only one to the
cold north.

For the " something else " was the children. Much
more interesting than the castle — indeed, what
would any castle or any house be without them?
Not that the castle was not a very interesting place
to live in, as you will hear, but all *places*, I think,
need people to bring out their interest. People who
have been, sometimes, and sometimes, people that
still are. There was a mixture of both in my castle.
But first and foremost I will tell you of the children,
whose home it was, and perhaps is yet.

There were only two of them, only two, that is to
say, who lived there regularly; they were girls, twin-
sisters, Ruby and Mavis were their names, and at
this time they were nearly twelve years old. I will
not say much in description of them, it is best to let
you find out about them for yourselves. They were

almost exactly the same size: Ruby perhaps a very little the taller, and at first sight every one thought them exceedingly like each other. And so they were, so far as the colour of their hair, the shape of their features, their eyes and complexions went. They were pretty little girls, and they made a pretty pair. But the more you got to know them the less alike you got to think them, till at last you began to wonder how you ever could have thought them like at all! And even almost at the first glance *some* differences were to be seen. Ruby was certainly the prettier. Her eyes were brighter, her colour more brilliant, her way of walking and holding herself more graceful, even her very manner of talking was more interesting and attractive.

"What a charming child she is," said strangers always. "Such pretty winning ways, so sweet and unselfish, so clever and intelligent! What a pity that dull little Mavis is not more like her — why, I thought them the image of each other at first, and now I can scarcely believe they are sisters. I am sure poor Ruby must find Mavis very trying, she is so stupid; but Ruby is so good and patient with her — it quite adds another charm to the dear child."

This opinion or one like it was always the first expressed — well, perhaps not *always*, but almost always. Now I will let you judge for yourselves.

It was late autumn. So late, that one felt inclined to wish it were already winter, without any thought or talk of a milder season. For it was very cold, and thick-walled though the castle was, it needed any amount of huge fires and curtains in front of the doorways and double windows, and, in the modern rooms, hot air or water-pipes to make it comfortable in severe weather. And all these things in winter it had. But the housekeeper had rather old-fashioned and stiff ideas. She did everything by rule. On a certain day in the autumn the winter arrangements were begun, on a certain day in the spring they came to an end. And this, whatever the weather was,— not a very good plan, for as everybody knows, the weather itself is not so formal and particular. There are quite warm, mild days sometimes in late November, and really bitterly cold ones in April and May. But there would have been no manner of use in trying to make old Bertha see this. Winter *should* stop on a certain day, and summer should come, and *vice versâ*. It had always been so in her time, and Bertha did not like new-fangled ways.

So everybody shivered, and the more daring ones, of whom Ruby was the foremost, scolded and grumbled. But it was no use.

"You may as well try to bear it patiently, my dear," said cousin Hortensia, "the mild weather must come soon. I will lend you one of my little shawls if you like. You will feel warmer when you have been out for a run."

Cousin Hortensia was the lady who lived at the

castle to teach and take care of the two little girls. For their mother was dead and their father was often away. He had some appointment at the court. I am not sure what it was, but he was considered a very important person. He was kind and good, as you will see, and it was always a great delight to the children when he came home, and a great sorrow when he had to leave.

Cousin Hortensia was only a very far-off cousin, but the children always called her so. For though she was really with them as a governess as well as a friend, it would not have seemed so nice to call her by any other name. She was very gentle, and took the best care she could of them. · And she was clever and taught them well. But she was rather a dreamy sort of person. She had lived for many years a very quiet life, and knew little of the outside world. She had known and loved the twins' mother, and their father too, when they were but boy and girl, for she was no longer young. And she loved Ruby and Mavis, Ruby especially, so dearly, that she could see no fault in them. It was to Ruby she was speaking and offering a shawl. They were sitting in one of the rooms on the south side of the castle, sheltered from the stormy winds which often came whirling down from the north. But even here it was cold, or at least chilly.

Ruby shrugged her shoulders.

"You always offer me a shawl as if I were seventy,

cousin Hortensia," she said rather pertly. "It would be much better if you would speak to Bertha, and *insist* on her having the fires lighted now it is so cold. When I'm grown up I can tell you *I* won't stand the old thing's tyranny."

Cousin Hortensia looked rather distressed. There was some sense in what Ruby said, but there were a great many other things to be considered, all of which she could not explain to the children. Bertha was an exceedingly valuable servant, and if she were interfered with and went away it would be almost impossible to get any one like her. For it was necessary that the castle should be managed with economy as well as care.

"I would speak to Bertha if there was anything really important to complain of," she said. "But this weather cannot last, and you are not cold at night, are you?"

"No," said Mavis, "not at all."

"Bertha would never get all the work done unless she took her own way," Miss Hortensia went on. "But I'll tell you what I'll do, Ruby. I will have the fire lighted in my own little room. I don't need to trouble Bertha about that, thanks to your kind father's thoughtfulness. My little wood-cupboard is always kept filled by Tim. And when you come in from your walk we will have tea there instead of here, and spend a cosy evening."

Ruby darted at Miss Hortensia and kissed her.

"That will be lovely," she said. "And as it's to be a sort of a treat evening, do tell us a story after tea, dear cousin."

"If you're not tired," put in Mavis. "Cousin Hortensia had a headache this morning," she said to Ruby, turning to her.

"Rubbish!" cried Ruby, but she checked herself quickly. "I don't mean that," she went on. "but Mavis is such a kill-joy. You won't be tired will you, dear cousin? Mavis doesn't care for stories as much as I do. I've read nearly all the books in the library, and she never reads if she can help it."

"I've enough to do with my lesson-books," said Mavis with a sigh. "And I can scarcely ever find stories to read that I understand. But I like *hearing* stories, for then I can ask what it means if there comes a puzzling part."

"Poor Mavis!" said Ruby contemptuously, "she's always getting puzzled."

"We must try to make your wits work a little quicker, my dear," said Miss Hortensia. "You will get to like reading when you are older, I dare say. I must look out for some easier story-books for you."

"But I love *hearing* stories, cousin," said Mavis. "Please don't think that I don't like your stories. I do so like that one about when you came to the castle once when you were a little girl and about the dream you had."

"I don't care for stories about dreams," said Ruby. "I like to hear about when cousin Hortensia was a young lady and went to balls at the court. I would love to have beautiful dresses and go to the court. Do you think father will take me when I'm grown up, cousin Hortensia?"

"I dare say he will. You will both go, probably," Miss Hortensia replied. "But you must not think too much of it or you may be disappointed. Your mother was very beautiful and everybody admired her when she went out in the world, but she always loved best to be here at the castle."

Ruby made a face.

"Then I don't think I'm like her," she said. "I'm very tired of this stupid old place already. And if you tell your dream-story to Mavis, you must tell *me* the one about how mother looked when she went to her first ball. She was dressed all in white, wasn't she?"

"No," Mavis answered. "In blue — wavy, changing blue, like the colour the sea is sometimes."

"*Blue*," Ruby repeated, "what nonsense! Isn't it nonsense, cousin Hortensia? Didn't our mother wear all white at her first ball — everybody does."

Miss Hortensia looked up in surprise.

"Yes, of course," she said. "Who ever told you she wore blue, Mavis?"

Mavis grew very red.

"I wasn't speaking of our mother," she said. "It

was the lady you saw in your dream I meant, cousin Hortensia."

"You silly girl!" said Ruby. "Isn't she stupid?"

Mavis looked ready to cry.

"You must get out of that habit of not listening to what people say, my dear," said Miss Hortensia. "Now you had better both go out — wrap up warmly, and don't stay very long, and when you come in you will find me in my own room."

"And you'll tell us stories, won't you, dear good cousin?" said Ruby coaxingly, as she put up her pretty face for a kiss. "If you'll tell me *my* story, you may tell Mavis hers afterwards."

"Well, well, we'll see," said Miss Hortensia, smiling.

"I do *so* like the story of the blue lady," said Mavis, very softly, as they left the room.

Five minutes later the twins were standing under the great archway which led to the principal entrance to the castle. At one end this archway opened on to a winding road cut in the rock, at the foot of which was a little sandy cove—a sort of refuge among the cliffs. On each side of it the waves broke noisily, but they never entirely covered the cove, even at very high tides, and except in exceedingly rough and stormy weather the water rippled in gently, as if almost asking pardon for intruding at all. When the sea was out there was a scrambling path among the rocks to the left, by which one could make one's way to a little fishing-hamlet about a quarter of a mile off on the west. For, as I should have explained before, the castle stood almost at a corner, the coast-line turning sharply southwards, after running for many miles almost due east and west.

The proper way to this hamlet was by the same inland road which led to the castle, and which, so the legend ran, was much more modern than the building itself, much more modern at least than the north side of it. That grim fortress-like front was very ancient. It had been built doubtless for a safe retreat, and originally had only been accessible from the sea, being in those days girt round on the land side by enormous walls, in which was no entrance of any kind. A part of these walls, ivy-clad and crumbling, still remained, but sufficient had been pulled down to give space for the pleasant sunny rooms and the sheltered garden with its terraces.

Ruby shivered as she and Mavis stood a moment hesitating in the archway.

"It is cold here," she said; "the wind seems to come from everywhere at once. Which way shall we go, Mavis?"

"It would be a little warmer at the back, perhaps," said Mavis. "But I don't care much for the gardens on a dull day like this."

"Nor do I," said Ruby, "there's nothing to see. Now at the front it's almost nicer on a dull day than when it's sunny — except of course for the cold. Let's go down to the cove, Mavis, and see how it feels there."

It was curious that they always spoke of the fortress side as the front, even though the southern part of the building was what would have naturally seemed so.

"I'd like to stay out till sunset and see the colours up in the turret windows," said Mavis, as they clambered down the rocky path. "I wish I knew which of these rooms is the one where the blue fairy lady used to come. I do think cousin Hortensia might have found out."

"Rubbish!" said Ruby. It was rather a favourite expression of hers, I am afraid. "I don't believe cousin Hortensia ever saw her. It was all a fancy because she had heard about it. If ever she did come, it was ages and ages ago, and I don't believe she did even then. I don't believe one bit about spirits and fairies and dreams and things like that."

Mavis said nothing, but a puzzled, disappointed look crept into her eyes.

"Perhaps it's because I'm stupid," she said, "but I shouldn't like to think like you, Ruby. And you know the story wouldn't have come all of itself, and cousin Hortensia, though she calls it a dream, can't really explain it that way."

"If you know so much about it, why do you keep teasing to have it told again?" said Ruby impatiently.

"Well, here we are at the cove; what are we to do now?"

Mavis looked about her. It was chilly, and the sky was gray, but over towards the west there was a lightening. The wind came in little puffs down here, now and again only, for they were well under the shelter of the cliffs. And up above, the old castle frowning down upon them — his own children, whose ancestors he had housed and sheltered and protected for years that counted by centuries — suddenly seemed to give a half unwilling smile. It was a ray of thin afternoon sunshine striking across the turret windows.

"See, see," said Mavis. "The sun's coming out. I'm sure the sky must be pretty and bright round where the cottages are. The sea's quite far enough back, and it's going out. Do let us go and ask how the baby — Joan's baby, I mean — is to-day."

"Very well," said Ruby. "Not that I care much how the baby is, but there's rather a nice scrambly way home up behind Joan's house. I found it one day when you had a cold and weren't with me. It brings you out down by the stile into the little fir-wood — just where you'd never expect to find your-self. And oh, Mavis, there's such a queer little cottage farther along the shore, at least just above the shore that way. I saw it from the back, along the scrambly path."

"I wonder whose it is," said Mavis. "I don't remember any cottage that way. Oh yes, I think I remember passing it one day long ago when Joan was our nurse, and she made me run on quick, but she didn't say why."

" Perhaps it's haunted, or some nonsense like that," said Ruby with her contemptuous air. " I'll ask Joan to-day. And if we pass it I'll walk just as slow as ever I can on purpose. You'll see, Mavis."

" We'd better run now," said Mavis. " The sands are pretty firm just here, and cousin Hortensia said we were to make ourselves warm. Let's have a race."

They had left the cove and were making their way to the hamlet by the foot of the rocks, where at low tide there was a narrow strip of pebbly sand, only here and there broken by out-jutting crags which the children found it very amusing to clamber over. Their voices sounded clear and high in the air. For the wind seemed to have fallen with the receding tide. By the time they reached the cottages they were both in a glow, and Ruby had quite forgotten her indignation at old Bertha's fireless rooms.

CHAPTER II.

WINFRIED.

                                    DRAYTON.

JOAN, a pleasant-faced young woman who had once been the children's nurse, and was now married to a fisherman who owned several boats, and was a person of some consequence among the villagers, was standing at the door of her cottage with a baby in her arms as the children came up. Her face beamed with smiles, but before she had time to speak Ruby called out to her.

"How are you, Joan? We've come round to ask how baby is, but it's very easy to see he is better, otherwise you wouldn't be so smiling."

"And here he is to speak for himself, Miss Ruby," said Joan. "How very kind of you to think of him! And you too, Miss Mavis, my dear. Are you both quite well?"

"Yes, thank you, Joan," said Mavis quietly. But Ruby was fussing about the baby, admiring him and petting him in a way that could scarcely fail to gain his mother's heart. Joan, however, though fond of both the children, had plenty of discernment. She smiled at Ruby — " Miss Ruby has pretty ways with her, there's no denying," she told her husband afterwards, — but there was a very gentle tone in her voice as she turned to Mavis.

" You've had no more headaches, I hope, Miss Mavis? Have you been working hard at your lessons?"

" I have to work hard if I work at all, Joan," said the little girl rather sadly.

" She's so stupid," said Ruby; "and she gets her head full of fancies. I dare say that prevents her having room for sensible things. Oh, by-the-bye, Joan, tell us who lives in that queer cottage all by itself some way farther along the coast. I never saw it till the other day — it's almost hidden among the rocks. But Mavis says she once passed it with you, and you made her run by quickly. Why did you, Joan? I do so want to know."

Joan looked rather at a loss.

" You mean old Adam's cottage," she said. " I really don't know why people speak against him. He's never done any harm, indeed, he's a kind old man. But he's come from a long way off, and he's not like the other folk, and they got up a tale that there were queer sounds and sights in his cottage sometimes — singing and lights late at night, that couldn't be canny. Some spoke of mermaids swimming down below in front of his hut and him standing talking to them quite friendly-like. But that's a good while ago now, and I think it's forgotten. And he goes to church regularly. You'll always be sure of seeing him there."

"Then why don't people like him?" said Mavis.

"Perhaps it's just because he is good and goes to church," said Ruby. "I'm not at all sure that I like extra good people myself. They're so tiresome."

"He's not one to meddle with others," said Joan. "He keeps very much to himself, and his talking doesn't sound like ours. So they call him a foreigner. Indeed, he's often not heard of or seen for weeks and even months at a time, unless any one's ill or in trouble, and then he seems to know it all of himself, and comes to see if he can help. That's one reason why they think him uncanny."

"Did he come when baby was ill?" asked Ruby.

Joan shook her head.

"No, for a wonder he didn't."

"Perhaps he's dead," said Ruby indifferently. "We're going past that way, Mavis. Let's peep in and see."

Mavis grew rather pale.

"Ruby," she said, "I wish you wouldn't — you frighten me."

"Miss Ruby would be frightened herself. She's only joking," said Joan. "I don't suppose there's aught the matter, still I don't think you'd better stop at old Adam's. It isn't like as if he was one of our own folk."

"Rubbish!" said Ruby again. "I'm off. You can send your husband to see if the old wizard has turned us into frogs or sea-gulls, in case we are not heard of any more. Good-night;" and off she ran.

Mavis had to follow her. There was not much fear of Ruby's really doing anything rash, for she was by no means a very brave child, still Mavis always felt uncomfortable when her sister got into one of these wild moods.

"Good-bye, Joan," she said gently. "I'm so glad baby's better. I dare say Ruby's only joking;" and then she ran along the path, which just here in the hamlet was pretty level and smooth, after Ruby.

They had quite half a mile to go before they got to the lonely cottage. It stood some way back from the shore, and great craggy rocks near at hand almost hid it from sight. One might have passed by that way often without noticing that there was any human dwelling-place there. But the children were on the look-out.

"There," said Ruby, "the old ogre can't be dead: there's smoke coming out of the chimney. And — oh, just look, Mavis, what a big fire he must have; do you see the red of it in the window?"

"No," said Mavis, "it's the sun setting. Look out to sea — isn't it splendid?"

But Ruby had set her heart upon exploring the

fisherman's hut. She began scrambling up the stones, for there was really nothing worthy of the name of a pathway, quite regardless of the beautiful sight behind her. And as usual, Mavis had to follow, though reluctantly. Still she was not quite without curiosity about the lonely cottage herself. Suddenly, when within a short distance of the hut, Ruby stopped short, and glancing back towards her sister, lifted her hand as if to tell her to be silent and listen. Then Mavis became conscious of the sound of voices speaking — not old Adam's voice certainly, for these sounded soft and clear, and now and then came a ripple of silvery laughter, very sweet and very delicate. The little girls, who had drawn near together, looked at each other.

"Who can it be?" said Mavis in a whisper.

"The mermaids," replied Ruby mockingly. "Perhaps old Adam has invited them to tea."

But as she spoke there came distinctly the sound of the words "Good-bye, good-bye," and then there was silence.

Somehow both children felt rather frightened.

"Suppose old Adam's really dead," said Ruby, looking rather pale, "and that these are — fairies, or I don't know what, come to fetch him."

"Angels," said Mavis. "Joan says he's good. But — Ruby — I shouldn't think angels would laugh."

She had scarcely said the words when they saw

running down the rough slope from the hut the figure of a boy. He ran fast and lightly, his feet scarcely seeming to touch the stones; he was slight and very active-looking; it was pretty to watch him running, even though as he came close it was plain that he was only a simple fisher-boy, in rough clothes, barefoot and sunburnt. He slackened his pace a little as he came near the children, then glancing at them with a smile he lifted his dark blue cap and stopped short.

"Can I — ?" he began, then hesitated. He had a pleasant face and clear gray eyes, which looked one straight in the face with interest and inquiry.

"What do you say?" asked Ruby rather haughtily.

"I thought perhaps you had lost your way," he answered quietly. "There's not many gentry comes round here;" and then he smiled, for no very particular reason apparently, though his smile nevertheless gave one the feeling that he had a reason if he chose to give it.

"No, we haven't lost our way," said Ruby; "we came here on purpose. Do you know the old man who lives up there?" and she pointed to the hut. "Is it true that there's something queer about him?"

The boy looked at her, still smiling.

"Queer?" he repeated.

Ruby began to feel annoyed. She tapped her foot impatiently.

"Yes," she said, "*queer*. Why do you repeat my

'Can I ——?' he began, then hesitated. P. 20

words, and why don't you say ‘Miss,’ or ‘My Lady’?
Lots of the people here call me ‘My Lady.’ Do you
know who I am?”

The boy's face had grown graver.

“Yes,” he said. “You are the little ladies from
the castle. I have seen you sometimes. I have seen
you in church. We always call you the little ladies
—grandfather and I—when we are talking. He
has told me about you — and — I've heard about the
castle, though I've never been in it. It's very fine. I
like to look up at it from the sea.”

Ruby felt a little smoothed down. Her tone became more gracious. Mavis, who had drawn near,
stood listening with great interest, and as the boy
turned towards her the smile came over his face
again.

“Who do you mean by ‘grandfather’?” asked
Ruby eagerly. “Is it old Adam? I didn't know
he had any children or grandchildren.”

“Yes,” the boy replied, “I'm his grandson. Was
it grandfather you meant when you said he was
queer?”

“Oh,” said Mavis, “Ruby didn't mean to be rude.
It was only nonsense. People say — ”

“They say he's very queer indeed,” said Ruby,
who had no intention of deserting her colours. “They
say he's a kind of a wizard or an ogre, and that you
hear all sorts of sounds — music and talking and I
don't know all what — if you're near his cottage in

the evening, and that there are lights to be seen in it too, not common lights like candles, but much more. Some say he's friends with the mermaids, and that they come to see him — is that true?" and notwithstanding her boasted boldness Ruby dropped her voice a little, and glanced over her shoulder half nervously seawards, as if not quite sure but that some of the tailed ladies in question might be listening to her.

The boy did more than smile now. He laughed outright; but his laugh, though bright and ringing, was not the laugh the sisters had heard from the cottage.

"The mermaids," he said. "No, indeed, poor little things, they never visit grandfather."

"Well, why do you laugh?" said Ruby angrily again. "You speak as if there *were* mermaids."

"I was thinking of stories I have heard about them," said the boy simply. "But I couldn't help laughing to think of them coming to see grandfather. How could they ever get up these stones?"

"Oh, I don't know, I'm sure," Ruby answered impatiently. "If he's a wizard he could do anything like that. I wish you'd tell us all about him. You must know, as you live with him."

"I've not been long with him," said the boy. "He *may* be friends with the mermaids for all I know. He's friends with everybody."

"You're mocking at me," said Ruby, "and I won't

have it. I'm sure you could tell me things if you chose."

"We did hear talking and laughing," said Mavis gently, speaking almost for the first time, "and it seemed as if there was some one else there."

The boy looked at her again, and a very pleasant light came into his eyes — more than that, indeed, as Mavis watched him it seemed to her that they changed in colour. Was it the reflection from the sky? No, there was a mingling of every hue to be seen over by the western horizon certainly, but scarcely the deep clear midsummer sky-blue they suddenly became.

"What funny eyes you've got," exclaimed the child impulsively. "They're quite blue now, and they weren't a minute ago."

Ruby stared at him and then at Mavis.

"Nonsense," she said, "they're not. They're just common coloured eyes. You shouldn't say such things, Mavis; people will think you're out of your mind."

Mavis looked very ashamed, but the boy's face flushed up. He looked both glad and excited.

"If you please, miss," he said, "some people see things that others don't. I don't even mind that nonsense about gran and the mermaids; those that say it don't know any better."

Ruby looked at him sharply.

"Then there is something to know," she said.

"Now you might as well tell us all about it. Is old Adam a wizard?"

"That he's not," answered the boy stoutly, "if so be, as I take it, that a wizard means one that has to do with bad spirits — unkind and mischief-making and unloving, call them what you will. None of such like would come near gran, or, if they did, he'd soon send them to the right-about. I'd like you to see him for yourself some day, but not to-day, if you'll excuse it. He's very tired. I was running down to the shore to fetch a pailful of sea water to bathe his lame arm."

"Then we mustn't keep you," said Mavis. "But might we really come to see your grandfather some day, do you think?"

"I'll ask him," said the boy; "and I think he'd be pleased to see you."

"You might come up to the castle if there's anything he would like — a little soup or anything," said Ruby in her patronising way. "I'll speak to the housekeeper."

"Thank you, miss," said the boy, but more hesitatingly than he had spoken before.

"What's your name?" asked Ruby. "We'd better know it, so that you can say who you are when you come."

"Winfried," he answered simply.

"Then good-bye, Winfried," said Ruby. "Come on, Mavis;" and she turned to pursue her way home past the cottage.

Winfried hesitated. Then he ran a step or two after them.

"I can show you a nearer way home to the castle," he said, "and if you don't mind, it would be very kind of you not to go near by our cottage. Grandfather is feeble still—did you know he had been very ill?—and seeing or hearing strangers might startle him."

"Then you come with us," said Ruby. "You can tell him who we are."

"I'm in a hurry to get the salt water," said the boy. "I have put off time already, and if you won't think me rude I'd much rather you came to the cottage some day when we could invite you to step in."

His manner was so simple and hearty that Ruby could not take offence, though she had been quite ready to do so.

"Very well," she said, "then show us your nearer way."

He led them without speaking some little distance towards the shore again. After all there was a path—not a bad one of its kind, for here and there it ran on quite smoothly for a few yards and then descended by stones arranged so as to make a few rough steps.

"Dear me," said Ruby, "how stupid we were not to find this path before."

Winfried smiled. "I scarce think you could have found it without me to show you," he said, "nor the short way home either for that matter. See here;" and having come to the end of the path he went on a few steps along the pebbly shore, for here there was no smooth sand, and stopped before a great boulder stone, as large as a hay-cart, which stood out suddenly among the broken rocks. Winfried stepped up close to it and touched it apparently quite gently. To the children's amazement it swung round lightly as if it had been the most perfectly hung door. And there before them was revealed a little roadway, wide enough for two to walk abreast, which seemed to wind in and out among the rocks as far as they could see. It was like a carefully rolled gravel path in a garden, except that it seemed to be of a peculiar kind of sand, white and glistening.

Ruby darted forward.

"What a lovely path!" she exclaimed: "will it take us straight home? Are you sure it will?"

"Quite sure," said Winfried. "You will see your way in no time if you run hand-in-hand."

"What a funny idea," laughed the child; and Mavis too looked pleased.

"I'm quite sure it's a fairy road," she was beginning to say, but, looking round, their little guide had disappeared. Then came his voice:

"Good-night," he said cheerfully. "I've shut-to the stone door, and I'm up on the top of it. Good-night, little ladies. Run home hand-in-hand."

The girls looked at each other.

"Upon my word," exclaimed Ruby, not quite knowing what to say, " if old Adam isn't a wizard his grandson is. I think we'd better get out of this as quick as we can, Mavis."

She seemed half frightened and half provoked. Mavis, on the contrary, was quite simply delighted.

" I shouldn't wonder if this was the mermaid's own way to the cottage," she said. " I'm sure old Adam and Winfried aren't wizards; but I do think they must be some kind of good fairies, or at least they must have to do with fairies. Come along, Ruby, hand-in-hand;" and she held out her own hand.

But Ruby by this time had grown cross.

" I won't give in to such rubbish," she said. " I don't want to go along hand-in-hand like two silly babies. If it was worth the trouble I'd climb up to the top of the stones and go home the proper way."

This was all boasting. She knew quite well she could not possibly climb up the stone. But she walked on a few steps in sulky dignity. Suddenly she gave a little cry, slipped, and fell.

" Oh, I've hurt my ankle!" she exclaimed. " This horrid white gravel is so slippery."

Mavis was beside her almost before she had said the words, and with her sister's help Ruby got on to her feet again, though looking rather doleful.

" I believe it's all a trick of that horrid boy's," she said. " I wish you hadn't made me come to see that dirty old cottage, Mavis."

Mavis stared.

"*Me* make you come, Ruby?" she said. "Why, it was yourself."

"Well, you didn't stop it, anyway," said Ruby, "and you seem to have taken such a fancy to that boy and his grandfather, and —"

"Ruby, we must go home," said Mavis. "Try if you can get along."

They were "hand-in-hand." There was no help for it now. Ruby tried to walk; to her surprise her ankle scarcely hurt her, and after a moment or two she even began urging Mavis to go faster.

"I believe I could run," she said. "Perhaps the bone in my ankle got out of its place and now has got into it again. Come on, Mavis."

They started running together, for in spite of her boasting Ruby had had a lesson and would not let go of Mavis. They got on famously; the ground seemed elastic; as they ran, each step grew at once firmer and yet lighter.

"It isn't a bit slippery now, is it?" said Mavis, glowing with the pleasant exercise. "And oh, Ruby, do look up at the sky — isn't it lovely? And isn't that the evening star coming out — that blue light up there; no, it's too early. See — no, it's gone. What could it be? Why, here we are, at the gate of the low terrace!"

They had suddenly, as they ran, come out from the path, walled in, as it were, among the broken rocky fragments, on to a more open space, which at the first moment they scarcely recognised as one of the fields at the south side of the castle.

Ruby too gazed about her with surprise.

"It *is* a quick way home, certainly," she allowed, "but I don't see any star or blue light, Mavis. It must be your fancy."

Mavis looked up at the sky. The sunset colours were just beginning to fade; a soft pearly gray veil was slowly drawing over them, though they were still brilliant. Mavis seemed perplexed.

"It is gone," she said, "but I did see it."

"It must have been the dazzle of the light in your eyes," said Ruby. "I am seeing lots of little suns all over — red ones and yellow ones."

"No, it wasn't like that," said Mavis; "it was more like —"

"More like what?" asked Ruby.

"I was going to say more like a forget-me-not up in the sky," said her sister.

"You *silly* girl," laughed Ruby. "I never did hear any one talk such nonsense as you do. I'll tell cousin Hortensia, see if I don't."

"I don't mind," said Mavis quietly.

CHAPTER III.

THE PRINCESS WITH THE FORGET-ME-NOT EYES.

Miss Hortensia was looking out for the little girls as they slowly came up the terraces.

"There you are at last," she called out. "You are rather late, my dears. I have been round at the other side, thinking I saw you go out that way."

"So we did," said Ruby. "We went down to the cove and along the shore as far as — Oh, cousin Hortensia, we have had *such* adventures, and last of all, what *do* you think? Mavis has just seen a forget-me-not up in the sky."

Miss Hortensia smiled at Mavis; she had a particular way of smiling at her, as if she was not perfectly sure if the little girl were quite like other people. But Mavis, though she understood this far better than her cousin imagined, never felt angry at it.

"A forget-me-not in the sky," said the lady; "that is an odd idea. But you must tell me all your adventures when we are comfortably settled for the evening. Run in and take your things off quickly, for I don't want you to catch cold, and the air, now the sun is set, is chilly. There is a splendid fire burning, and we shall have tea in my room as I promised you."

"Oh, how nice," said Ruby. "Come along, Mavis. I'm as hungry as a hawk."

"And you'll tell us stories after tea, cousin Hortensia, won't you?" said Mavis: "at least you'll tell us about your queer dream."

"And about mamma's going to court," added Ruby, as she dashed upstairs. For by this time they were inside the house.

The part of the castle that the children and their cousin and the few servants in attendance on them occupied was really only a corner of it. A short flight of stairs led up to a small gallery running round a side-hall, and out of this gallery opened their sleeping-rooms and what had been their nursery and play-rooms. The school-room and Miss Hortensia's own sitting-room were on the ground-floor. To get to any of the turrets was quite a long journey. They were approached by the great staircase which ascended from the large white and black tiled hall, dividing, after the first flight, into two branches, each of which led to passages from which other smaller stairs went upwards to the top of the house. The grandest rooms opened out of the tiled hall on the ground-floor, and out of the passages on the first floor. From this central part of the house the children's corner was shut of by heavy swing doors seldom opened.

So when Ruby and Mavis visited the turrets they had to pass through these doors, and go some way along the passages, and then up one of the side stairs — up, up, up, the flights of steps getting steeper and narrower as they climbed, till at last they reached the door of the turret-chamber itself. Of these chambers there were two, one in each turret, east and west. The west was their favourite, partly because from it they saw the sunset, and partly because it was nearer their own rooms. They had been allowed to make a sort of private nest of it for themselves, and to play there on rainy days when they could not get out, and sometimes in very cold or snowy weather they had a fire there, which made the queer old room very cheery. There were three windows in each turret, and they were furnished in an odd, irregular way with all sorts of quaint old-fashioned furniture discarded from other parts of the castle. In former days these turret-rooms had some-times been used as guest-chambers when the house was very full of visitors. For the large modern rooms and the hall I have spoken of had been added by the children's grandfather — a very hospitable but extravagant man. And before he made these im-provements there were often more guests than it was easy to find room for.

Ruby and Mavis were not long in taking off their out-door things and "tidying" themselves for their evening in Miss Hortensia's pleasant little room. They made a pretty picture as they ran downstairs, their fair curls dancing on their shoulders, though if I were to describe to you how they were dressed, I am afraid you would think they must have been a very old-world looking little pair.

"Here we are, cousin Hortensia," exclaimed Ruby as they came in, "and I do hope it's nearly tea-time."

"Not quite, my dear," Miss Hortensia replied, glancing at a beautifully carved Swiss clock which stood on the mantelpiece; "the little trumpeter won't tell us it's six o'clock for half an hour yet — his dog has just barked twice."

"Lazy things," said Ruby, shrugging her shoulders, "I'd like to shake that old trumpeter sometimes."

"And sometimes you'd like to pat him to sleep, wouldn't you?" said Mavis. "When cousin Hortensia's telling us stories, and he says it's bed-time."

Miss Hortensia looked at Mavis in some surprise, but she seemed very pleased too. It was not often Mavis spoke so brightly.

"Suppose you use up the half-hour in telling *me* stories," said their cousin. "Mine will keep till after tea. What were all the adventures you met with?"

"Oh," said Ruby, "it was too queer. Did you know, cousin, that there was a short way home from the sea-shore near old Adam's cottage? *Such* a queer way : " and she went on to describe the path between the rocks.

Miss Hortensia looked very puzzled.

"Who showed it to you?" she said: for Ruby, in her helter-skelter way, had begun at the end of the story, without speaking of the boy Winfried, or explaining why they — or she — had been so curious about the old man whom the villagers called a wizard.

"It was the boy," Mavis replied: "such a nice boy, cousin Hortensia, with funny bluey eyes — at least they're *sometimes* blue."

"Oh, Mavis, do not talk so sillily," said Ruby; "his eyes aren't a bit blue. She's got blue on the brain, cousin, she really has. Seeing forget-me-nots in the sky too! I don't think he *was* a particularly nice boy. He was rather cool. I'm sure we wouldn't have done his grandfather any harm. Did you ever hear of him, cousin? Old Adam they call him;" and then she went on to give a rather more clear account of their walk, and all they had seen and heard.

Miss Hortensia listened attentively, and into her own eyes crept a dreamy, far-away, or rather long-ago look.

"It is odd," she said; "I have a kind of fancy

that I have heard of the old 'solitary,' for he must be almost a hermit, before. But somehow I don't think it was here. I wonder how long he has lived here?"

"I don't know," said Ruby. "A good while, I should think. He was here when Joan was our nurse."

"But that was only two years ago," said Miss Hortensia, smiling. "If he had been here many years the people would not count him so much of a foreigner. And the boy you met — has he come to take care of the old man?"

"I suppose so. We didn't ask him," said Ruby carelessly. "He was really such a cool boy, ordering us not to go near the cottage indeed! I told him he might come up to get some soup or jelly for his grandfather," she went on, with a toss of her head. "I said it, you know, just to put him in his place, and remind him whom he was speaking to."

"I'm sure he didn't mean to be rude," said Mavis; "and, cousin, there really was something rather 'fairy' about him. Isn't it *very* queer we never heard of that path before?"

"Yes," Miss Hortensia replied. "Are you sure you didn't both fall asleep on the shore and dream it all? Though, to be sure, it is rather too cold weather for you to have been overcome by drowsiness."

"And we couldn't both have dreamt the same

thing if we had fallen asleep," said Mavis, in her practical way. "It wasn't like when you were a little girl and saw or dreamt —"

"Don't you begin telling the story if cousin Hortensia's going to tell it herself," interrupted Ruby. "I was just thinking I had forgotten it a good deal, and that it would seem fresh. But here's tea at last — I am so glad."

They were very merry and happy during the meal. Ruby was particularly pleased with herself, having a vague idea that she had behaved in a very grand and dignified way. Mavis's eyes were very bright. The afternoon's adventure had left on her a feeling of expecting something pleasant, that she could hardly put in words. And besides this, there was cousin Hortensia's story to hear.

When the table was cleared, cousin Hortensia settled herself with her knitting in a low chair by the fire, and told the children to bring forward two little stools and seat themselves beside her. They had their knitting too, for this useful art had been taught them while they were so young that they could scarcely remember having learnt it. And the three pairs of needles made a soft click-click, which did not the least disturb their owners, so used were they to it. Rather did it seem a pleasant accompaniment to Miss Hortensia's voice.

"You want me to tell you the story of my night in the west turret-room when I was a little girl," she began. "You have heard it before, partly at least, but I will try to tell it more fully this time. I was a very little girl, younger than you two — I don't think I was more than eight years old. I had come here with my father and mother and elder sisters to join a merry party assembled to celebrate the silver wedding of your great-grandparents. Your grandfather himself, their eldest child, was about three and twenty. He was not then married, so it was some time before your father was born. I don't quite know why they had brought me. It seems to me I would have been better at home in my nursery, for there were no children as young as I to keep me company. Perhaps it was that they wished to have me to represent another generation, as it were, though, after all, that might have been done by my sisters. The elder of them, Jacintha, was then nineteen; it was she who afterwards married your grandfather, so that besides being cousins of the family, as we were already, I am your grandmother's sister, and thus your great-aunt as well as cousin."

The little girls nodded their heads.

"I was so much younger than Jacintha," Miss Hortensia went on, "that your father never called me aunt. He and I have always been Robert and Hortensia to each other, and to me he has always been like a younger brother."

"But about your adventure," said Ruby, who was not of a sentimental turn.

"I am coming to it," said their cousin. "Well, as I said, the party was a merry one. They had dancing and music in plenty every evening, and the house, which was in some ways smaller than it is now, was very full. There were a great many bedrooms, though few of them were large, and I and my sisters, being relations, were treated with rather less ceremony than some of the stranger guests, and put to sleep in the turret-room. I had a little bed in one corner, and my sisters slept together in the same old four-poster which is still there. I used to be put to bed much earlier than they came, for, as I said, there were dancing and other amusements most evenings till pretty late. I was not at all a nervous or frightened child, and even sometimes when I lay up there by myself wide awake — for the change and the excitement kept me from going to sleep as quickly as at home — I did not feel at all lonely. From my bed I could see out of the window, for the turret windows are so high up that it has never been necessary to have blinds on them, and I loved to lie there watching the starlit sky, or sometimes, when the moon was bright and full, gazing up at the clouds that went scurrying over her face. One night I had been unusually wakeful. I lay there, hearing now and then very, very faint, far-off sounds of the music down below. It was a mild night, and I think the windows were a little open. At last I must have fallen asleep. When I awoke, or rather when I *thought* I awoke, the room was all in darkness except in one corner, the corner by the west window. There, there was a soft steady light, and it seemed to me that it was on purpose to make me look that way. For there, sitting on the old chair that still stands in the depth of that window was some one I had never seen before. A lady in a cloudy silvery dress, with a sheen of blue over it. My waking, or looking at her, for though it must all have been a dream, I could not make you understand it unless I described it as if it were real, seemed to be made conscious to her, for she at once turned her eyes upon me, then rose slowly and came over the room towards me."

"Weren't you frightened?" said Ruby breathlessly. In spite of her boasted disbelief in dreams and visions her cousin's story had caught her attention. Miss Hortensia shook her head.

"Not in the *very* least," she said. "On the contrary, I felt a strange and delightful kind of pleasure and wonder. It was more intense than I have ever felt anything of the kind in waking life; indeed, if it had lasted long I think it would have been more than I could bear —" Miss Hortensia stopped for a moment and leant back in her chair. "I have felt *something* of the same," she went on, "when listening to very, *very* beautiful music — music that seemed too beautiful and made you almost cry out for it to stop."

"I've never heard music like that," whispered little Mavis, "but I think I know what you mean."

"Or," continued Miss Hortensia, "sometimes on a marvellously beautiful day — what people call a "heavenly" day, I have had a feeling rather like it. A feeling that makes one shut one's eyes for very pleasure."

"Well," said Ruby, "did you shut your eyes then, or what did you do?"

"No," said her cousin. "I could not have shut them. I felt she was looking at me, and her eyes seemed to catch and fasten mine and draw them into hers. It was her eyes above all that filled me with that beautiful wonderful feeling. I can never forget it — never. I could fancy sometimes even now, old woman as I am, that I am again the little enraptured child gazing up at the beautiful vision. I feel her eyes in mine still."

"How funny you are," interrupted Ruby. "A minute ago you said she pulled your eyes into hers, now you say hers came into yours. It would be a very funny feeling whichever it was; I don't think I should like it."

Miss Hortensia glanced at her, but gravely. She did not smile.

"It must be a very 'funny' feeling, as you call it, to a hitherto blind man the first time he sees the sunshine. I dare say he would find it difficult to describe; and to a still blind person it would be impossible to explain it. I dare say the newly-cured man would not feel sure whether the sun had come into his eyes or his eyes had reached up to the sun."

Ruby fidgeted.

"Oh, do go on about the fairy or whatever she was," she said. "Never mind about what I said."

Miss Hortensia smiled.

"The lady came slowly across the room to me," she went on, "and stood by my bed, looking down at me with those wonderful blue eyes. Then she smiled, and it seemed as if the light about her grew still brighter. I thought I sat up in bed to see her better. 'Are you a fairy?' I said at last. She smiled still more. 'If you like, you may call me a fairy,' she answered. 'But if I am a fairy my home must be fairyland, and this turret-room is one of my homes. So you are my guest, my little girl.' I did not mind her saying that. I smiled too. 'I've never seen you here before,' I said. And she laughed a little — I never heard anything so pretty as her laugh. 'No,' she replied, 'but I have seen you and every one that has ever been here, though every one has not seen me. Now listen, my child. I wanted you to see me because I have something to say to you. There will come a time when you will be drawn two ways, one will be back here to the old castle by the sea, after many years; many, many years, as you count things. Choose that way, for you will be wanted here. Those yet unborn will want you, for they will want love and care. Look into my eyes, little girl, and promise me you will come to them.' And in my dream I thought I gazed again into her eyes, and I felt as if their blue light was the light of a faith and truth that could not be broken, and I said, 'I promise.' And then the fairy lady seemed to draw a gauze veil over her face, and it grew dim, and the wonderful eyes were hidden, and I thought I fell asleep. In reality, I suppose, I had never been awake."

"And when you did wake up it was morning, I suppose, and it had all been a dream?" asked Ruby.

Miss Hortensia gave a little sigh.

"Yes," she said, "I suppose it had been a dream. It was morning, bright morning, the sun streaming in at the other window when I awoke, and I never saw the fairy lady again — not even in a dream. But what she had said came true, my dears. Many, many years after, when I was already beginning to be an old woman, it came true. I am afraid I had grown selfish — life had brought me many anxieties, and I had lived in a great city where there was much luxury and gaiety, and where no one seemed to have thought for anything but the rush of pleasure and worldly cares. I had forgotten all about my beautiful vision, when one day there came a summons. Your sweet young mother had died, my darlings, and your poor father in his desolation could think of no one better to come and take care of his little girls

—you were only two years old——than his old cousin. And so I came; and then there crept back to me the remembrance of my dream. I had indeed been drawn two ways, for the friends I might have gone to live with were rich and good-natured, and they promised me everything I could wish. But I thought of the two little motherless ones, here in the old castle by the sea, in want of love and care as *she* had said, and I came."

Miss Hortensia stopped. Even Ruby was impressed by what she had heard.

"Dear cousin," she said, "it was very good of you."

"And have you never seen the beautiful lady again?" said Mavis. "She told you the west turret was her own room, didn't she? Have you never seen her there?"

Miss Hortensia shook her head.

"You forget, dear, it was only a dream. And even if it had been more than that, we grow very far away from angels and fairies as we get old, I fear."

"Not *you*," Mavis said; "you're not like that. And the lady must have been so pleased with you for caring for us, I wonder she hasn't ever come to see you again. Do you know," she went on eagerly, after a moment's pause, "I have a feeling that she *is* in the west turret-room sometimes!"

Miss Hortensia looked at the child in amazement.

Mavis's quiet, rather dull face seemed transformed: it was all flushed and beaming, her eyes sparkling and bright.

"Mavis!" she said, "you look as if you had seen her yourself. But it was only a dream, you mustn't let my old-world stories make you fanciful. I am too fanciful myself perhaps — I have always loved the west turret, and that was why I chose it for your play-room when you were little dots."

"I'm so glad you did," said Mavis, drawing a long breath.

After that they were all rather silent for a while. Then Ruby claimed Miss Hortensia's promise of the story or description rather of the grand court ball at which her mother's beauty had made such a sensation, and when that was ended, the little trumpeter announced, much to the children's displeasure, that it was time to go to bed.

"We *have* had a cosy evening," said Mavis, as she kissed Miss Hortensia.

"And, oh Ruby," she said, as her sister and she were going slowly upstairs, "*don't* you wish we might sleep in the turret-room?"

"No indeed," Ruby replied, in a most decided tone, "I certainly don't."

CHAPTER IV.

A BOY AND A BOAT.

"If you please, there's a boy at the kitchen-door asking for the young ladies," said the young maid-servant Ulrica, who generally waited on Ruby and Mavis.

They were just finishing their morning lessons with Miss Hortensia, and Mavis was putting away the books, a task which usually fell to her share.

Miss Hortensia gave a little start.

"A boy," she exclaimed, "what kind of a boy? It can't be — oh no of course not. How foolish I am. At the kitchen-door, did you say, Ulrica? Who is it?"

"Oh, I know!" cried Ruby, jumping up with a clatter, delighted to avoid finding out the mistake in a sum which Miss Hortensia had told her she must correct. "It's Winfried; I'm sure it is. He's come for some soup or something. I told him he might, but I do think it's rather greedy to have come the very next day. Mayn't I go and speak to him, cousin?"

"Well, yes, I suppose so.   No, I think it would be better for him to come in here.   Show the boy in here, Ulrica — at least — ask him if he is old Adam's grandson."

In a minute or two the door was again opened.

"If you please, ma'am," said Ulrica's voice as before, "it's — it's the boy."

"The boy" walked in; he held his cap in his hand, and made a sort of graceful though simple obeisance to the ladies. He did not seem the least shy, yet neither was there a touch of boldness about him.   On his face was the slight but pleasant smile that had more than once lighted it up the day before, and his eyes, as he stood there full in the bright gleam of the window — for it was a clear and sunny day — were *very* blue.

Ruby came forward.

"Oh, it's you, is it?" she said, with the half-patronising good humour usual to her when not put out.   "I thought it was.   It's Winfried, cousin Hortensia; the boy I told you of.   I suppose you've come for some soup for your grandfather."

Winfried smiled, a little more than before.   Mavis crept forward; she wished she could have said something, but she was afraid of vexing Ruby.

"No, miss," said Winfried, "I did not come for that, though grandfather said it was very kind of you, and some day perhaps —" he stopped short. "I came to bring you this which I found on the rocks down below our cottage;" and he held out a little silver cross. Ruby started, and put her hand up to her neck.

"Oh dear," she said, "I never knew I had lost it. Are you sure it isn't yours, Mavis? I've got my cord on."

"Yes, but the cross must have dropped off," said Mavis. "I have mine all right."

And so it proved. Both little sisters wore these crosses, which were exactly alike. Ruby took hers from Winfried, and began examining it to see how it had got loose. Miss Hortensia came forward.

"It was very good of you to bring the little cross," she said kindly; for something about the boy attracted her very much. "Ruby, my dear," she went on half reprovingly. Ruby started and looked up. "I am sure you are very much obliged?"

"Oh yes, of course I am," said the little girl carelessly. "It certainly was very sharp of you to find it," she added with more interest.

"I can generally find things," said Winfried quietly.

"Is there anything we can do for your grandfather?" asked Miss Hortensia. "I am sorry to hear he's so ill."

The boy shook his head; a sad look passed across his bright face.

"Yes," he said, "he's pretty bad sometimes. But some days he's much better. He's better to-day.

There's one thing he would like," he went on, "he told me to ask you if some day the young ladies might come to see him; he said I might ask —"

Ruby interrupted —

"Why, how funny you are," she said; "that was just what we wanted yesterday, and you wouldn't let us go near the cottage. You said we'd startle him."

"He was very tired yesterday," said Winfried; "and you see he wasn't looking for you."

"He was chattering and laughing all the same — or somebody was," said Ruby. "We heard them — don't you remember?"

Winfried did not speak. But he did not seem vexed.

"I believe it was the mermaids after all," Ruby went on. "Cousin Hortensia, if you let us go there the mermaids will steal us."

"No, indeed," exclaimed Winfried eagerly.

Miss Hortensia smiled at him.

"I am not afraid," she said. "Tell your grandfather the young ladies shall certainly go to see him some day soon."

"To-morrow," said Mavis, speaking almost for the first time. "Oh, do say we may go to-morrow — it's our half-holiday."

"Very well," said Miss Hortensia. "Are you sure you can find your way? I can send Ulrica with you."

" Mayn't I come to fetch the young ladies?" asked Winfried. " I know all the short cuts."

" I should think you did," laughed Ruby. " We told cousin Hortensia all about that queer path through the rocks. *She'd* never seen it either."

" I'll take you quite as nice a way to-morrow," said the boy composedly. " May I go now please?" he added, turning to Miss Hortensia. " Grandfather may be wanting me, and thank you very much;" and in another moment he was gone.

Miss Hortensia was quite silent for a minute or two after he had left the room.

" Cousin," began Ruby; but her cousin did not seem to hear. " *Cousin*," repeated the child impatiently.

Miss Hortensia looked up as if awakened from a brown study.

" Did you speak, my dear?" she said.

" Yes, of course I did. I want you to say something about that queer boy. I suppose you think him very nice, or you wouldn't let Mavis and me go to his cottage. You're generally so frightened about us."

" I do think he is a very nice boy," said Miss Hortensia. " I am sure he is quite trustworthy."

" *I* believe he's a bit of a fairy, and I'm sure his old grandfather's a wizard," murmured Ruby. " And I quite expect, as I said to Joan, that we shall be turned into sea-gulls or frogs if we go there."

"I shouldn't mind being a sea-gull," said Mavis. "Not for a little while at least. Would you, cousin Hortensia?"

But Miss Hortensia had not been listening to their chatter.

"My dears," she said solemnly, "I will tell you one reason why I should be glad for you sometimes to have Winfried as a companion if he is as good and manly as he seems. I have had a letter from your father, telling me of a new guest we are to expect. It is a cousin of yours — a little nephew of your father's — your aunt Margaret's son. He is an only child, and, your father fears, a good deal spoilt. He is coming here because his father is away at sea and his mother is ill and must be kept quiet, and Bertrand, it seems, is very noisy."

"Bertrand," repeated Ruby, "oh, I remember about him. I remember father telling us about him — he is a horrid boy, I know."

"Your father did not call him a horrid boy, I'm sure," said Miss Hortensia.

"No," said Mavis, "he only said he was spoilt. And he said he was a pretty little boy, and nice in some ways."

"Well, we must do our best to make him nicer," said Miss Hortensia; "though I confess I feel a little uneasy — you have never been accustomed to rough bearish ways. And if Winfried can be with you sometimes he might help you with Bertrand."

"When is he coming?" asked Ruby.

"Very soon, but I do not know the exact day. Now run off, my dears; there is time for you to have half an hour's play in the garden before dinner."

It was curious that of the two little girls Mavis seemed the more to dislike the idea of the expected guest.

"Ruby," she said rather dolefully, "I do wish Bertrand weren't coming. He'll spoil everthing, and we shan't know what to do with him."

"There's not much to spoil that I see," said Ruby. "What do you mean?"

"Oh, our nice quiet ways. Cousin Hortensia telling us stories and all that," said Mavis. "And I'm sure Winfried won't want to have to look after a rough, rude little boy. It's quite different with *us* — Winfried likes us because we're — ladies, you know, and gentle and nice to him."

Ruby laughed.

"How you go on about Winfried — Winfried!" she said mockingly. "I think it's a very good thing Bertrand is coming to put him down a bit — a common fisher-boy! I wonder at cousin Hortensia. I'm sure if father knew he wouldn't be at all pleased, but *I'm* not going to tell him. I mean to have some fun with Master Winfried before I have done with him, and I expect Bertrand will help me."

"Ruby!" exclaimed Mavis, looking startled, "you don't mean that you are going to play him any tricks?"

Ruby only laughed again, more mockingly than before.

"I'd like to lock him up in the haunted room in the west turret one night," she said. "I do hope he'd get a good fright."

Mavis seemed to have recovered from her alarm.

"I don't believe he'd mind the least scrap," she said; "that shows you don't understand him one bit. He'd like it; besides, you say yourself you think he's a fairy boy, so why should he be afraid of fairies?"

"Nobody's afraid of *fairies*, you silly girl. But if cousin Hortensia saw anything in the turret — and I don't believe she did. — it wasn't a fairy, it was quite different — more a sort of witch, I suppose."

"You're always talking of witches and wizards," retorted Mavis, who seemed to be picking up a spirit which rather astonished Ruby. "*I* like thinking of nicer things — angels and — oh Ruby!" she suddenly broke off, "do look here — oh, how lovely!" and stooping down she pointed to a thick cluster of turquoise blossoms, almost hidden in a corner beneath the shrubs. *Aren't* they darlings? Really its enough to make one believe in fairies or kind spirits of some kind — to find forget-me-nots like these in November!" and she looked up at her sister with delight dancing in her eyes.

Even Ruby looked surprised.

"They are beauties," she said; "and I'm almost sure they weren't there yesterday. Didn't we come round by here, Mavis?"

'—Oh Ruby!' she suddenly broke off, 'do look here — oh, how lovely!'

P. 52

"Not till it was nearly dark. We ran in this way, you know, after we came out of Winfried's path," said Mavis.

"Oh, yes, I remember," Ruby replied, and a half dreamy look stole over her face.

They were standing on the lower terrace. This side of the castle, as I have said, was much more sheltered and protected than the other, but still already in November it was bleak and bare. The evergreen shrubs had begun to look self-satisfied and important, as I think they always do in late autumn, when their fragile companions of the summer are shivering together in forlorn misery, or sinking slowly and sadly, leaf by leaf, brown and shrivelled, into the parent bosom of Mother Earth, always ready to receive and hide her poor children in their day of desolation. Nay, more, far more than that does she for them in her dark but loving embrace; not a leaf, not a tiniest twig is lost or mislaid — all, everything, is cared for and restored again, at the sun's warm kiss to creep forth in ever fresh and renewed life and beauty. For all we see, children dear, is but a type, faint and shadowy, of the real things that *are*.

Then a strange sort of irritation came over Ruby. The soft wondering expression so new to her disappeared, and she turned sharply to Mavis.

"Rubbish!" she said. "Of course they were there yesterday. But they shan't be there to-morrow — here goes;" and she bent down to pick the little flowers.

Mavis stopped her with a cry.

"Don't gather them, Ruby," she said. "Poor little things, they might stay in their corner in peace, and we could come and look at them every day. They'd wither so soon in the house."

Ruby laughed. She was much more careless than actually unkind, at least when kindness cost her little.

"*What* a baby you are," she said contemptuously. "You make as much fuss as when I wanted to take the thrush's eggs last spring. Wouldn't you like to give your dear Winfried a posy of them?"

"No," Mavis answered, "he wouldn't like us to gather them; there are so few and they do look so sweet."

The next day was clear and bright, but cold; evidently winter was coming now. But old Bertha had started the fires at last, as the date on which it was the rule at the castle for them to begin on was now past. So inside the house it was comfortable enough — in the inhabited part of it at least; though in the great unused rooms round the tiled hall, where all the furniture was shrouded in ghostly-looking linen covers, and up the echoing staircase, and up still higher in the turret-rooms where the wind whistled in at one window and out again at the opposite one, where Jack Frost's pictures lasted the same on the panes for days at a time — dear, dear, it *was* cold, even Bertha herself allowed, when she had to make her weekly tour of inspection to see that all was right.

"I will ask Miss Hortensia not to let the little ladies play in the west turret this winter," thought the old woman. "I'm sure it was there Miss Mavis caught her cold last Christmas. A good fire indeed! It'd take a week of bonfires to warm that room."

But old Bertha was mistaken, as you will see.

There was no thought of playing in the west turret this half-holiday, however, for it was the right sort of day for a bright winter walk. And while the afternoon was still young, Ruby and Mavis, warmly wrapt up in their fur-lined mantles and hoods, were racing downstairs to Winfried, who had come punctually and was waiting for them, so Ulrica had come in to say, at the door in the archway on the sea side of the castle.

"What are you here for?" was Ruby's first greeting. "Why didn't you come to the garden side? Aren't you going to take us by the path between the rocks, down below the field?"

"No, Miss Ruby," said the boy, his cap in his hand. "We're going another way to-day. I think you will like it just as well. We must go down to the cove first."

"*I* don't mind," said Ruby, dancing on in front of the two others; "but I'm afraid Mavis has been dreaming of that nice cosy little path. She wouldn't let me even look for the entrance to it yesterday; she said we should wait for you to show it us."

"I think Miss Mavis will like to-day's way just as well." Winfried repeated.

They were some little distance down the cliff by this time. It was very clear and bright; for once, the waves, even though the tide was close up to the shore, seemed in a peaceful mood, and only as a distant murmur came the boom of their dashing against the rocks, round to the right beyond the little sheltered nook. Winfried stood still for a moment and gazed down seawards, shading his eyes with his hand, for winter though it was, the after-noon sunshine was almost dazzling.

"What is it? What are you looking for?" asked Ruby, coming back a step or two and standing beside him. "Do come on; it's too cold to hang about."

For once Winfried was less polite than usual. He did not answer Ruby, but turned to Mavis, who was a little behind.

"Do you see anything?" he asked.

And Mavis, following his eyes, answered, "Yes — there's — oh, there's a little boat drifting in — a tiny boat — *is* it drifting? No; there's some one in it, — some one with a blue cloak; no, it must have been the waves just touching; the waves are so blue to-day."

The boy gave a little sigh of satisfaction.

"I thought so," he said. Then he sprang forward eagerly: "Come on," he cried, "we mustn't be late."

Ruby followed, not too pleased.

"I've as good eyes as Mavis," she said. "Why didn't you ask me? I don't believe there's a boat at all."

But even Ruby had to give in when in a few minutes they found themselves at the edge of the cove, on the little half-circle of sand which was all that the sea left uncovered at full tide. For there *was* a boat, a most unmistakable and delightful boat, though scarcely larger than a sofa, and looking like a perfect toy as it rocked gently on the rippling water.

"Goodness!" said Ruby,—and it must be allowed that goodness is a prettier word than rubbish,—"how in the world did that boat come here? Did you bring it, Winfried? No, for if you had you wouldn't have been looking to see if it had come. But is it your boat?"

"No," answered the boy; "it's lent me, on purpose for you and Miss Mavis. Get in, please."

Ruby came forward, but hesitated.

"Are you sure it's safe?" she said. "You know the sea is very rough — round there near the village. And this is such a very little boat."

Winfried laughed.

"It's as safe as — as the safest thing you can think of," he said. "*You're* not afraid, Miss Mavis."

For all answer the little girl sprang into the boat; it danced under her feet, but she only laughed.

"Come on, Ruby," she called out: "it's lovely."

Ruby stepped in cautiously. The little boat was

most dainty and pretty. There were cushions for the little girls, and one or two soft rich coloured shawls, of a fashion and material such as they had never seen before.

"Dear me," said Ruby, settling herself in the most comfortable place and drawing the pretty rugs round her, "what a nice little boat! Your friends must be very rich, Winfried. But I know what I know;" and she shook her head mysteriously.

"What do you mean, Ruby?" said Mavis.

Winfried was busy with his oars and did not seem to be attending to them. Ruby leant forward and whispered, close into her sister's ear, "*Mermaids!*" Then seeing or thinking that the boy was not listening, she went on. "You know mermaids *are* very rich. They dive down into the shipwrecked vessels and fish up all the treasures. I dare say these shawls have come from some strange country, right over at the other side of the world. Indeed, *some* people say that the horrid things sing to make the sailors turn to look for them and get their ships all in among the rocks."

Mavis looked puzzled.

"I don't think that's *mermaids*," she said. "There's another name for those naughty, unkind creatures."

"Syrens," came Winfried's voice from the other end of the boat. And he looked up with a smile at the little girls' start of surprise. "Don't be afraid," he said, "my friends are neither mermaids nor syrens;

you're not going to be shipwrecked in this boat, I promise you."

Somehow the boy seemed to have gained a new kind of dignity now that the children were, so to say, his guests. Ruby said, "Thank you," quite meekly and submissively for her.

Then they were all quite silent for a while, only the plash of Winfried's oars broke the stillness. And somehow out there on the water it seemed to have grown warmer, at least the children felt conscious of neither cold nor heat, it was just perfectly pleasant. And the sun shone on mildly. There was a thorough feeling of "afternoon," with its quiet and mystery and yet faint expectation, such as one seldom has except in summer.

"It is lovely," said Mavis presently; "only I'm a little afraid I'm getting sleepy."

"No, you needn't be afraid," said Winfried; and just as he said the words, Mavis started, as something flitted against her cheek.

"Ruby, Ruby!" she exclaimed, "did you see it? A butterfly — a blue butterfly — in November! Oh, where has it gone to?" and she gazed all round anxiously.

CHAPTER V.

THE FISHERMAN'S HUT.

". . . There are things which through the gazing eye
Reach the full soul and thrill it into love."

To my Child.

Ruby burst out laughing.

" You've been asleep and dreaming, you silly girl,"
she said. " Winfried, do you hear? Mavis says a
blue butterfly flew past."

" It kissed my cheek," said Mavis.

Winfried smiled: " It's quite possible," he said.

Ruby was just turning upon him with her laughter,
when something made *her* jump in turn. Something
cold and damp touched her hand: she had taken her
glove off and was dabbling idly in the water.

" Ugh," she said, " I do believe that was a toad."

The laugh was against her now.

" A toad, Ruby, out at sea! What are you thinking of?" said Mavis. " You needn't make fun of my
butterfly if you talk of toads."

" Well, it was something slimy and horrid like a
toad," said Ruby. " Perhaps it was only a fish. But
whatever it was, I believe it was a trick of Winfried's.
I'm sure, positive sure, you're a wizard, Winfried."

She was half in fun and half in earnest. But the boy took it quite composedly.

"No, I'm not," he said; "and no more is gran. But — people don't understand, you see. If they see that one's a bit different from others they've no words for it but wizard and uncanny, and they get frightened when it should be just the other way."

This was much more of a speech than the fisher-boy was in the habit of making. Both the children listened with interest.

"How is your gran different from others?" asked Ruby.

"You'll see it in his face; at least, I think you will," said Winfried. "But now I mustn't talk, we're close to the little creek."

He got the boat in most cleverly, to a very tiny creek, where was a little landing-place, and leading upwards from it a flight of steps cut in the rock.

"How funny, how very funny we never saw this place before," exclaimed the little girls. "Do you keep the boat here, Winfried?"

"Sometimes," he replied, "but not to-day. We won't need it again."

He folded up the shawls and laid them neatly on the cushions, then he drew in the oars, and in another moment he had helped the children to get on shore, and all three had mounted several of the rock steps when Winfried called to them to stop for a moment.

"Look down," he said; and as he spoke, the little

girls saw something moving there below where they had just landed. It was the little boat; calmly and steadily it was moving out to sea, though it had no sails, and the oars were lying just as Winfried had drawn them in.

"O Winfried," exclaimed Ruby; "the dear little boat, it's drifting out, it will be lost. Can't you jump into the water and drag it back?"

"It's all right," said the boy. "It's going home till it's needed again. I only wanted you to see how quietly it goes off, once its business is done."

And he turned and began to whistle softly as he went on up the steps.

"*Now*," said Ruby, half triumphant and half frightened, in a whisper to Mavis, "*now*, can you say he's not a wizard? I think cousin Hortensia was very silly to let us come with him, but it was all you, Mavis, going on about him so. If we're not turned into toads or lizards before we get home, I —"

"Butterflies would be nicer," said Mavis, laughing. "I'll ask Winfried and his gran to make me into a blue butterfly, and you can be a yellow one if you like."

She seemed to have caught something of Winfried's happy confidence. Ruby looked at her in surprise, but it was mixed with anger. What she was going to have said I don't know, for just then their guide called out again.

"Here we are," he said, "if you'll stoop your

heads a little;" and looking up, the children saw before them a narrow, low archway, at the entrance to which the steps stopped. Ruby hung back a little, but Mavis ran forward.

"It's all right, Ruby," she called back; "and oh, what a pretty garden! Do come quick."

Ruby followed. It was only necessary to stoop for a moment or two, then she found herself beside her sister, and she could not help joining in her exclamation of pleasure. Somehow or other they had arrived at the back of the cottage, which at this side, they now saw, stood in a pretty and sheltered garden. Perhaps garden is hardly the word to use, for though there were flowers of more than one kind and plants, there were other things one does not often see in a garden. There were ever so many little bowers and grottoes, cleverly put together of different kinds of queerly-shaped and queerly-coloured fragments of rock; there were two or three basins hollowed out of the same stones, in which clear water sparkled, and brilliant seaweed of every shade, from delicate pink to blood-red crimson, glowed; there were shells of strange and wonderful form, and tints as many as those of the rainbow, arranged so that at a little distance they looked like groups of flowers — in short, Ruby was not far wrong when returning to her old idea, she whispered to Mavis, "It's a *mermaid's* garden. And I only hope," she went on in the same tone, "we shan't find that somehow or other he has got us down under the sea without our knowing."

Mavis broke into a merry laugh.

"Don't be afraid," she said. "Look up; there's the good old sun, smiling as usual, with no water between him and us. And see here, Ruby," and she ran forward, "there are earth flowers too, as well as sea ones."

She was right; on a border sheltered by the wall of the cottage were great masses of fern, still green and luxuriant, and here and there among them clumps, brilliantly blue, of the tender, loving forget-me-not.

"It's *just* like that bunch of it we found on our terrace," said Mavis, joyfully. "I really could believe you had brought a root of it and planted it there for us, Winfried. I never saw such beauties."

"Gran loves it," was all the boy said. Then he led them round to the front of the house, and opened the door for them to enter.

Inside the cottage all was very plain, but very, very neat and clean. In an old-fashioned large wooden arm-chair by the fire sat old Adam. He looked very old, older than the children had expected, and a kind of awe came over them. His hair was white, but scarcely whiter than his face, his hands were unusually delicate and refined, though gnarled and knotted as are those of aged people. He looked up with a smile, for his sight was still good, as his visitors came in.

"You will forgive my not standing up, my dear little ladies," he said. "You see I am very old. It is good of you to come to see me. I have often seen you, oftener than you knew, since you were very tiny things."

"Have you lived here a long time, then?" asked Ruby.

"It would seem a long time to you, though not to me," he said with a smile. "And long ago before that, I knew your grandmother and the lady who takes care of you. When I was a young man, and a middle-aged man too for that matter, my home was where theirs was. So I remember your mother when she was as little as you."

"Oh, how nice," exclaimed Mavis. "Was our mother like us, Mr. Adam?"

"You may be very like her if you wish," he said kindly.

But their attention was already distracted. On a small table, close beside the old man's chair, in what at first sight looked like a delicate china cup, but was in reality a large and lovely shell, was a posy, freshly gathered apparently, of the same beautiful forget-me-nots.

"Oh, these are out of your garden," said Ruby; "how do you manage to make them grow so well and so late in the year?"

"The part of the garden where they grow is not mine," said Adam quietly; "it belongs to a friend who tends it herself. I could not succeed as she does."

"Is — is she a mermaid?" asked Ruby, her eyes growing very round.

"No, my dear. Mermaids' flowers, if they have any, would scarcely be like these, I think."

"You speak as if there are no such things as mermaids; do you not think there are?" said Mavis.

Old Adam shook his head.

"I have never seen one; but I would never take upon myself to say there is nothing but what I've seen."

"Tell us about the friend who plants these in your garden," said Ruby, touching the forget-me-nots. "Could it have been she who put some on the terrace at the castle for us?"

"Maybe," said the old man.

"Is she a lady, or — or a fairy, or what is she, if she's not a mermaid?" asked Ruby.

Before the old man could answer, Winfried's voice made her start in surprise.

"She's a princess," he said; and he smiled all over his face when he saw Ruby's astonishment.

"Oh!" was all she said, but her manner became more respectful to both Adam and his grandson from that moment.

Then the old man made a sign to Winfried, and the boy went out of the room, coming back in a moment with a little plain wooden tray, on which were two glasses of rich tempting-looking milk and a basket of cakes, brown and crisp, of a kind the children had never seen before. He set the tray down on a table which stood in the window, and Adam begged the children to help themselves.

They did so gladly. Never had cake and milk tasted so delicious. Ruby felt rather small when she thought of her condescending offer of soup from the castle kitchen.

"But then," she reflected, "of course I didn't know — how could I ? — that a princess comes to see them. I dare say she sends them these delicious cakes. I wish Bertha could make some like them."

"I never saw cakes like these before," said little Mavis. "They are *so* good."

Old Adam seemed pleased.

"My boy isn't a bad cook," he said proudly, with a glance at Winfried.

"Did *you* make them?" said Ruby, staring at Winfried. "I thought perhaps as a princess comes to see you that *she* sent you them — they are so very good."

Winfried could not help laughing: something in Ruby's speech seemed to him so comical.

Then at the little girls' request he took them out again to examine some of the wonders of the grotto-garden. He fished out some lovely sprays of sea-weed for them, and gave them also several of the prettiest shells; best of all, he gathered a sweet nosegay of the forget-me-nots, which Mavis said she would take home to cousin Hortensia. And then, as the sun by this time had travelled a long way downwards, they ran in to bid old Adam good-bye, and to thank him, before setting off homewards.

"How are we going?" asked Ruby. "You've sent away the boat."

"I could call it back again, but I think we had better go a shorter way," said Winfried. "You're not frightened of a little bit of the dark, are you? There's a nice short cut to the rock path through one of the arbours."

The little girls followed him, feeling very curious, and, perhaps, just a tiny scrap afraid. He led them into one of the grottoes, which, to their surprise, they found a good deal larger than they had expected, for it lengthened out at the back into a sort of cave. This cave was too dark for them to see its size, but Winfried plunged fearlessly into its recesses.

"I must see that the way is clear," he said, as he left them; "wait where you are for a few minutes."

Ruby was not very pleased at being treated so unceremoniously.

"I don't call waiting here a quick way of getting home," she said, "and I hate the dark. I've a good mind to run out and go back the regular way, Mavis."

"Oh no," Mavis was beginning, but just then both

children started. It seemed to have grown suddenly dark outside, as if a cloud or mist had come over the sky; and as they gazed out, feeling rather bewildered, a clear voice sounded through the grotto.

"Ruby; Mavis," it said.

Ruby turned to Mavis.

"It's a trick of that boy's," she said. "He wants to startle us. He has no business to call us by our names like that. I'll not stay;" and she ran out. Mavis was following her to bring her back when a ray of light — scarcely a ray, rather, I should say, a soft glow — seemed to fill the entrance to the grotto. And gradually, as her eyes got used to it, she distinguished a lovely figure — a lady, with soft silvery-blue garments floating round her and a sweet grave face, was standing there looking at her. A strange thrill passed through the child, yet even as she felt it she knew it was not a thrill of fear. And something seemed to draw her eyes upwards — a touch she could not have resisted if she had wished — till they found their resting-place in meeting those that were bent upon her — those beautiful, wonderful blue eyes, eyes like none she had ever seen, or — nay, she had *heard* of such eyes — they were like those of the fairy lady in her old cousin's dream. And now Mavis knew in part why the strange vision did *not* seem strange to her; why, rather, she felt as if she had always known it would come, as if all her life she had been expecting this moment.

"Mavis," said the soft yet clear and thrilling voice, "you see me, my child?"

"Yes," said the little girl, speaking steadily, though in a whisper, "I see you, and I see your eyes. Who are you? I may ask you, may I not?"

The fairy — if fairy she was — smiled.

"I have many names," she said; "but if you like you may think of me by the one Winfried loves. He calls me 'Princess with the Forget-me-not Eyes,' or 'Princess Forget-me-not.'"

"Yes," said Mavis, "I like that; and I will never forget you, princess."

Again the lovely vision smiled.

"No, my child, you never will, for to tell you a secret, you cannot, even if you wished. Afterwards, when you know me better, you will see how well my name suits me. But it does not seem to all a sweet name, as I think it always will to you," and she sighed a little. "There are those who long to forget me; those who wish they had never seen me."

The sadness in her eyes was reflected in the child's.

"How can that be?" asked Mavis.

The blue-eyed princess shook her head.

"Nay, my darling, I cannot tell you, and I scarce would if I could," she said gently. But then a brighter look came over her face again. "Don't look so sad. They change again some of them, and seek me as earnestly as they would have before fled from

'Mavis,' said the soft yet clear and thrilling voice, 'you see me, my child?'

P. 70

me. And some day you may help and guide such seekers, simple as you are, my little Mavis. Now I must go — call Ruby — she would not stay for me; she has not yet seen me. But she heard my voice, that is better than nothing. Good-bye, little Mavis, and if you want me again before I come of myself, seek me in the west turret."

Mavis's face lighted up.

"Then it *was* you — you are cousin Hortensia's fairy, and it wasn't a dream after all. And of course you must be a fairy, for that was ever, ever so long ago. She was a little girl then, and now she is quite old, and you look as young as — as —"

"As who or what?" asked the princess, smiling again.

"As the Sleeping Beauty in the wood," replied Mavis, after deep consideration.

At this the princess did more than smile; she laughed, — the same clear delicate laugh which the children had heard that day in the distance.

And Mavis laughed too; she could not help it.

"May I tell cousin Hortensia?" she asked. "Oh do say I may."

"You may," said Forget-me-not, "if — if you *can*."

And while Mavis was wondering what she meant, a breath of soft wind seemed to blow past her, and glancing up, the princess was gone!

Mavis rubbed her eyes. Had she been asleep? It seemed a long time since Winfried told her and Ruby to wait for him in the grotto; and where was Ruby? Why did she not come back? Mavis began to feel uneasy. Surely she had been asleep — for — was she asleep still? Looking round her, she saw that she was no longer in the grotto-cave behind old Adam's cottage, but standing in the archway at the sea side of the castle — the archway I have told you of into which opened the principal entrance to the grim old building. And as she stood there, silent and perplexed, uncertain whether she was not still dreaming, she heard voices coming near. The first she could distinguish was Ruby's.

"There you are, Mavis, I declare," she exclaimed. "Now it's too bad of you to have run on so fast without telling, and I've been fussing about you all the way home, though Winfried said he was sure we should find you here. How *did* you get back?"

"How did *you?*" asked Mavis in return. "And why didn't you come back to me in the grotto? I — I waited ever so long, and then —" but that was all she could say, though a smile broke over her face when she thought of what she had seen.

"You look as if you had been asleep," said Ruby impatiently.

"And having pleasant dreams," added Winfried. "But all's well that ends well. Won't you run in now, my little ladies, and let Miss Hortensia see that I've brought you safe back. It is cold and dark standing out here, and I must be off home."

"Good-night, then," said Ruby: "you're a very queer boy, but you brought *me* home all right anyway, and those cakes were very good."

"You will come to see us soon again, won't you, Winfried?" said Mavis, who felt as if she had a great deal to ask which only he could answer, though with Ruby there beside her she could not have explained what she wanted to know.

"To be sure I will, if you want me," said the boy. "Don't be puzzled, Miss Mavis, pleasant dreams don't do any one harm."

And as they pushed open the great, nail-studded door which was never locked till after nightfall, Winfried ran off.

They stood still for a moment just inside the entrance. They could hear him whistling as he went, smoothly at first, then it seemed to come in jerks, going on for a moment or two and then suddenly stopping, to begin again as suddenly.

"He's jumping down the cliff. I can hear it by his whistle," said Ruby. "How dangerous!"

"He's very sure-footed," said Mavis with a little sigh. She was feeling tired — and — *was* it a dream? If so, how had she got home? Had the fairy lady wrapped her round in her cloak of mist and flown with her to the castle? Mavis could not tell, and somehow Ruby did not ask her again.

"How did you come home, Ruby?" Mavis asked as they were going along the passage to their sitting-room.

"Oh," said Ruby, "Winfried took me down some steps, and then up some others, and before I knew where we were, we were in the rock path not far from home. It was like magic. I can't make out that boy," she said mysteriously; "but we're not turned into frogs or toads *yet*. Here we are, cousin Hortensia," she went on, as the good lady suddenly appeared at the end of the passage, "safe home from the wizard's haunts."

But Miss Hortensia only smiled.

"I was not uneasy," she said. "I thought you would be quite safe."

CHAPTER VI.

BERTRAND.

THEY were just beginning tea, and Ruby's tongue
was going fast as she described to Miss Hortensia all
that happened that afternoon, while Mavis sat half-
dreamily wondering what the fairy lady had meant
by saying she might tell her cousin about her " if she
could," when there came a sudden and unusual
sound that made them all start. It was the clanging
of the great bell at the principal entrance on the
south side — the entrance by which, you remember,
all visitors, except those coming by sea, came to the
castle.

" Who can that be ? " exclaimed Ruby, jumping up
and looking very pleased — Ruby loved any excitement. " Can it be father ? What fun if he's come
to surprise us ! Only I hope he won't have forgotten
our presents. He generally asks us what we want
before he comes."

Mavis had grown a little pale; somehow the

things that Ruby was frightened of never alarmed her, and yet she was more easily startled by others that Ruby rather enjoyed.

"I hope it isn't a message to say that anything is the matter with dear father," she said anxiously.

Miss Hortensia got up from her seat and went to the door. She did not seem frightened, but still rather uneasy.

"I'm afraid," she began, "I'm afraid — and yet I should not speak of it that way; it is not kind. But I did so ask them to give us notice of his coming."

She had left the room almost before she had finished speaking. The children looked at each other.

"I say, Mavis," said Ruby, "it's Bertrand! Don't you think we might run out and see?"

"No." Mavis replied decidedly, "certainly not. Cousin Hortensia would have told us to come if she had wanted us."

But they went to the open door and stood close beside it, listening intently. Then came the sound of old Joseph's steps along the stone passage from the part of the house which he and Bertha — Joseph was Bertha's husband — inhabited, then the drawing back of the bolts and bars, and, most interesting and exciting of all, a noise of horses stamping and shaking their harness as if glad to have got to the end of their journey. Then followed voices; and in a minute or two the children heard Miss Hortensia coming back, speaking as she came.

"You must be very cold, my dear boy, and hungry too," she was saying. "We are just beginning tea, so you had better come in at once as you are."

"It's terribly cold, and that fool of a driver wouldn't come any faster; he said his horses were tired. I wish *I* could have got a cut at them — what are horses for?" was the reply to Miss Hortensia's kind speech.

Mavis touched Ruby.

"Come in. Cousin Hortensia wouldn't like to see us standing at the door like this," she said.

They sat down at their places again, only getting up as Miss Hortensia came in.

She was followed by a boy. He was about the height of the twins, broad and strong-looking, wrapped up in a rich fur-lined coat, and with a travelling cap of the same fur still on his head. He was dark-haired and dark-eyed, a handsome boy with a haughty, rather contemptuous expression of face — an expression which it did not take much to turn into a scowl if he was annoyed or put out.

"These are your cousins, Bertrand; your cousins Ruby and Mavis — you have heard of them, I am sure, though you have never met each other before."

Bertrand looked up coolly.

"I knew there were girls here," he answered. "Mother said so. But I don't care for girls — I told mother so. I'm awfully hungry;" and he began to pull forward a chair.

"My dear," said Miss Hortensia, "do you know you have not taken off your cap yet? You must take off your coat too, but, above all, your cap."

Bertrand put up his hand and slowly drew off his cap.

"Mother never minds," he said. But there was a slight touch of apology in the words.

Then, more for his own comfort evidently than out of any sense of courtesy, he pulled off his heavy coat and flung it on to a chair. The little girls had not yet spoken to him, they felt too much taken aback.

"Perhaps he is shy and strange, and that makes him seem rough," thought Mavis, and she began drawing forward another chair.

"Will you sit here?" she was saying, when Bertrand pushed past her.

"I'll sit by the fire," he said, and he calmly settled himself on what he could not but have seen was her seat or Ruby's: "and I'm awfully hungry," he went on. "At home I have dinner, at least if I want it, I do. It's only fit for girls to have tea in this babyish way."

He helped himself to a large slice of cake as he spoke; and not content with this, he also put a big piece of butter on his plate. Miss Hortensia glanced at him, and was evidently just going to speak, but checked herself. It was Bertrand's first evening, and she was a very hospitable person. But when Bertrand proceeded to butter his cake thickly. Ruby, never accustomed to control her tongue, burst out.

"That's cake, Bertrand," she said. "People don't butter *cake*."

"Don't they just?" said the boy, speaking with his mouth full. "*I* do, I know, and at home mother never minds."

"Does she let you do whatever you like?" asked Ruby.

"Yes," said Bertrand; "and whether she did or not I'd do it all the same."

Then he broke into a merry laugh. It was one of the few attractive things about him, beside his good looks, that laugh of his. It made him seem for the time a hearty, good-tempered child, and gave one the feeling that he did not really mean the things he said and did. And now that his hunger was appeased, and he was warm and comfortable, he became much more amiable. Ruby looked at him with admiration.

"I wish I lived with your mother," she said, "how nice it must be to do always just what one likes!"

"Do you think so?" said Mavis. "I think it would be quite miserable."

"Quite right, Mavis," said Miss Hortensia. "When I was a child I remember reading a story of a little girl who for a great treat one birthday was allowed to do just what she wanted all day, and — oh dear! — how unhappy she was before evening came."

Bertrand stared at her with his big eyes. *Some eyes are very misleading*; his looked now and then as if he had nothing but kind and beautiful thoughts behind them.

"What a fool she must have been," he said roughly. And poor Miss Hortensia's heart sank.

The evening was not a long one, for Bertrand was tired with his journey, and for once willing to do as he was told, by going to bed early. A room near his cousins' had been preparing for him, and though not quite ready, a good fire made it look very cosy. They all went upstairs with him to show him the way. As they passed the great baize door which divided their wing from the rest of the house, Bertrand pushed it open.

"What's through there?" he asked, in his usual unceremonious way.

"Oh, all the rest of the castle," said Ruby importantly.

Bertrand peered through. It was like looking into a great church with all the lights out, for this door opened right upon the gallery running round the large hall.

"What a ramshackle old cavern!" said Bertrand. A blast of cold air rushed in through the doorway as he spoke and made them all shiver.

"Nonsense, Bertrand," said Miss Hortensia, more sharply than she had yet spoken to him. "It is a splendid old house."

"You should see the staircases up to the turrets,"
said Ruby. "They are as high as — as I don't know
what. If you are naughty we can put you to sleep
in the west turret-room, and they say it's haunted."

"*I* shouldn't mind that," laughed Bertrand.

"Nor should I," said Ruby boastfully. "Mavis
here is a dreadful coward. And — oh, Bertrand —
I'll tell you something to-morrow. I have such an
idea. Don't you love playing tricks on people —
people who set themselves up, you know, and preach
at you?"

Her last words were almost whispered, and Miss
Hortensia, who had gone on in front — they had
closed the swing door by this time — did not hear
them. But Mavis caught what Ruby said, and she
waited uneasily for Bertrand's answer.

"Prigs, you mean," he said. "I hate prigs. Yes,
indeed, I'll join you in any game of that kind. You
should have seen how we served a little wretch at
school who tried to stop us teaching a puppy to swim
— such a joke — the puppy could scarcely walk,
much less swim. So we took Master Prig and made
him swim instead. It was winter, and he caught a
jolly cold, and had to leave school."

"Did he get better?" said Mavis, in a strange voice.

"Don't know, I'm sure. I should think not. His
mother was too poor to pay for a doctor, they said.
He'd no business to be at school with gentlemen,"
said Bertrand brutally.

Mavis gasped. Then suddenly, without saying good-night to any one, she rushed down the passage to the room she shared with her sister: and there Ruby found her a few minutes later on her knees and all in the dark.

"What's the matter with you? Cousin Hortensia told me to say good-night to you for her. It wasn't very civil to fly off like that the first night Bertrand was here. I'm sure cousin Hortensia thought so too," said Ruby carelessly. "My goodness, are you *crying?*" as the light she carried fell on Mavis's tear-stained face.

"Cousin Hortensia didn't *hear*," said Mavis. "Oh, Ruby, I can't bear it."

"What?"

"That wicked boy. Oh, Ruby, you can't say you like him?"

"I think he's lots of fun in him," said Ruby wonderingly. "He's only a boy: you are so queer, Mavis." But catching sight again of her sister's expression she suddenly changed. "Poor little Mavie," she cried, throwing her arms round her, "you're such a goose. You're far too tender-hearted."

Mavis clung to her, sobbing.

"Oh, Ruby, my Ruby," she said, "don't speak like that. I couldn't *bear* you to get hard and cruel."

But Ruby was, for her, wonderfully gentle and

kind, and at last the two little sisters kissed each other, promising that nothing should ever come between them.

A good night's rest and a huge breakfast put Master Bertrand into a very fairly amiable humour the next morning. He flatly refused, however, to do any lessons, though it was intended that he should; and Miss Hortensia, judging it best to make a virtue of necessity, told him he should have his time to himself for three days, after which he must join the twins in the school-room.

"For these three days," she said, "I will give Ruby and Mavis a half-holiday, so that they may go about with you and show you everything. But if you do not come regularly and punctually to lessons after that, I will not give your cousins any extra holidays while you are here."

She spoke firmly, and Bertrand looked at her with surprise. He was surprised indeed into unusual meekness, for he said nothing but "All right."

They gave him some directions as to where he would be most likely to amuse himself and with safety. Indeed, unless one were *determined* to hurt oneself, there were no really dangerous places about the castle; in spite of the cliffs and the sea, Ruby and Mavis had played there all their lives without ever getting into mischief.

"He is not a stupid boy," said Miss Hortensia, after giving her instructions to Bertrand, "and I have no doubt he can take care of himself if he likes."

"I'm sure he wouldn't like to hurt himself," said Ruby with a little contempt; "he's the sort of boy that would hate pain or being ill."

"It is to be hoped nothing of that kind will happen while he is here," said Miss Hortensia. "But I can only do my best. I did not seek the charge, and it would be quite impossible to shut him up in the house."

"He'd very likely try to get out of the window if you did, cousin Hortensia," said Mavis with her gentle little laugh. She was feeling happy, for Ruby had continued kind and gentle this morning. "And if I were a boy I'm not sure but that I would too, if I were shut up."

"Well, let us get to our work," said Miss Hortensia with a resigned little sigh.

Lessons were over; Ruby and Mavis had had their usual morning run along the terrace, had brushed their hair and washed their hands, and were standing up while Miss Hortensia said grace before beginning dinner, when Bertrand appeared.

He came banging in, his cap on his head, his boots wet and dirty, his cheeks flushed, and his eyes bright with running and excitement. He looked very pretty notwithstanding the untidy state he was in, but it was impossible to welcome him cordially; he was so rude and careless, leaving the door wide open, and bringing in a strong fishy smell, the reason of which was explained when he flung down a great mass of course slimy seaweed he had been carrying.

"You nasty, dirty boy," said Ruby, turning up her nose and sniffling.

"Really, Bertrand, my dear," began Miss Hortensia, "what have you brought that wet seaweed here for? It cannot stay in this room."

"I'll take it away," said Mavis, jumping up.

"What harm does it do?" said Bertrand, sitting down sideways on his chair. "I want it. I say you're not to go pitching it away, Mavis. Well, when am I to have something to eat?"

"Go and wash your hands and hang up your coat and come and sit straight at the table and then I will give you your dinner," said Miss Hortensia drily.

"Why can't you give it me now?" said Bertrand, with the ugly scowl on his face.

"Because I will not," she replied decidedly.

The roast meat looked very tempting, so did the tart on the sideboard. Bertrand lounged up out of his seat, and in a few minutes lounged back again. Eating generally put him into a better temper. When he had got through one plateful and was ready for another, he condescended to turn to his companions with a more sociable air.

"I met a fellow down there — on the shore," he

said, jerking his head towards where he supposed the sea to be; "only a common chap, but he seems to know the place. He was inclined to be cheeky at first, but of course I soon put him down. I told him to be there this afternoon again; we might find him useful, now he knows this place."

Ruby's eyes sparkled.

"I'm very glad you did put him down," she said. "All the same—" then she hesitated.

"Do you know who he is?" asked Bertrand.

"He's the best and nicest and cleverest boy in all the world," said little Mavis.

Bertrand scowled at her and muttered something of which "a dirty fisher-boy," was all that was audible. Miss Hortensia's presence did overawe him a little.

"I am afraid there can be no question of any of you going out this afternoon," she said, glancing out of the window as she spoke: "it is clouding over—all over. You must make up your minds to amuse yourselves indoors. You can show Bertrand over the house—that will take some time."

"May we go up into the turret-rooms and everywhere?" said Ruby.

"Yes, if you don't stay too long. It is not very cold, and you are sure to keep moving about. There—now comes the rain."

Come indeed it did, a regular battle of wind and water; one of the sudden storms one must often expect on the coast. But after the first outburst the sky grew somewhat lighter, and the wind went down a little, the rain settling into a steady, heavy pour that threatened to last several hours. For reasons of her own, Ruby set herself to coax Bertrand into a good humour, and she so far succeeded that he condescended to go all over the castle with them, even now and then expressing what was meant to be admiration and approval.

"It isn't ramshackle, anyway," said Ruby. "It's one of the strongest built places far or near."

"If I were a man and a soldier, as I mean to be," said Bertrand boastfully, "I'd like to cannonade it. You'd see how it'd come toppling over."

"You wouldn't like to see it, I should think," said Mavis. "It's been the home of your grandfathers just as much as of ours. Don't you know your mother is our father's sister?"

Bertrand stared at her.

"What does it matter about old rubbishing grandfathers and stuff like that?" he said. "That was what that fisher-fellow began saying about the castle, as if it was any business of his."

"Yes indeed," said Ruby, "he's far too fond of giving his opinion." She nodded her head mysteriously. "We'll have a talk about him afterwards, Bertrand."

"Ruby," began Mavis in distress; but Ruby pushed her aside.

"Mind your own business," she said, more rudely than Mavis had ever heard her speak.

"It's all Bertrand," said Mavis to herself, feeling ready to cry. "I'm sure they are going to plan some very naughty unkind thing."

They were on their way up the turret-stair now; the west turret. They had already explored the other side. Suddenly a strange feeling came over Mavis; she had not been in this part of the castle since the adventure in the grotto.

"She said she comes to the west turret still," thought the child; "just as she did when cousin Hortensia was a little girl. I wonder if she only comes in the night? I wonder if possibly I shall see her ever up here? If I did, I think I would ask her to stop Bertrand making Ruby naughty. I am sure dear Princess Forget-me-not *could* make anybody do anything she liked."

And she could not help having a curious feeling of expecting something, when Ruby, who was in front, threw open the turret-room door.

"This is the *haunted* room, Bertrand," she said, and there was a mocking tone in her voice. "At least so Mavis and cousin Hortensia believe. Cousin Hortensia can tell you a wonderful story of a night she spent here if you care to hear it."

Bertrand laughed contemptuously.

"I'd like to see a ghost uncommonly," he said. "It would take a good lot of them to frighten *me*."

"That's what I say," said Ruby. "But the room looks dingy enough, doesn't it? I don't think I ever saw it look so dingy before."

" It looks as if it was full of smoke," said Bertrand, sniffing about ; " but yet I don't smell smoke."

There *was* something strange. Mavis saw it too, and much more clearly than did the others. To her the room seemed filled with a soft blue haze; far from appearing "dingy," as Ruby said, she thought the vague cloudiness beautiful ; and as she looked, it became plain to her that the haze all came from one corner, where it almost seemed to take form, to thicken and yet to lighten : for there was a glow and radiance over there by the window that looked towards the setting sun that did not come from any outside gleam or brightness. No indeed. For the rain was pouring down, steadily and hopelessly, with dull pitiless monotony from a leaden sky. Scarcely could you picture to yourself a drearier scene than the unbroken gray above, and unbroken gray beneath, which was all there was to be seen from the castle that afternoon. Yet in Mavis's eyes there was a light, a reflection of something beautiful and sunshiny, as she stood there gazing across the room, with an unspoken hope in her heart.

The others did not see the look in her face, or they saw it wrong, Ruby especially, strange to say.

"What are you gaping at, Mavis?" she said. " You do look so silly."

Bertrand stared at her in his turn.

"She looks as if she was asleep, or dreaming," he said curiously.

Mavis rubbed her eyes.

"No, no," she said brightly, "I'm not."

And then she tried to be very kind and merry and pleasant to the others. She felt as if "somebody" was watching, and would be pleased. And Bertrand was a little bit gentler and softer than he had yet been, almost giving Mavis a feeling that in some faint far-off way the sweet influence was over him too.

But Ruby was very contradictory. She ran about making fun of the old furniture and mocking at Miss Hortensia's story till she got Bertrand to join with her, and both began boasting and talking very foolishly — worse than foolishly indeed. More than once Mavis caught words and hints which filled her with distress and anxiety. She knew, however, that when Ruby was in this kind of humour it was less than useless to say anything, now above all that she had got Bertrand to back her up.

Suddenly the boy gave an impatient exclamation.

"I hate this cockloft," he said. "It's so stuffy and choky, and that smoke or mist has got into my eyes and makes them smart. Come along, Ruby, do."

"It's not stuffy. I think it's dreadfully cold," she replied. "But I'm sure I don't want to stay here.

The mist's quite gone — not that I ever saw any really; it was only with the room being shut up, I suppose. I'm quite ready to go; let's run down and get a good warm at the school-room fire, and I'll tell you something — a grand secret, Bertrand."

CHAPTER VII.

IN THE TURRET-ROOM.

"The wind with the clouds is battling,
Till the pine-trees shriek with fear."
PAN.

THEY ran off, leaving Mavis alone in the turret-room. Poor Mavis! all her happy and hopeful feelings were gone.

"It is no use," she said to herself; "I can't stop Ruby. Bertrand will just make her as naughty as himself. Oh, *how* I do wish he had never come! All our happiness is spoilt."

And feeling very sorry for herself, and for every one concerned except Bertrand, towards whom, I fear, her feelings were more of anger than grief, Mavis sat down on one of the capacious old chairs that stood beside her and began to cry quietly. Suddenly a strange sensation came over her — through her, rather. She drew her handkerchief from her eyes and looked up — she *had* to look up — and — yes, there it was again, there *they* were again. The wonderful unforgetable blue eyes, so searching, so irresistible, so tender. Sweet and perfectly loving as they were, it was yet impossible to meet them without a half-trembling thrill. And the first thought that flashed through the little girl was. "How could I bear her to look at me if I had been naughty?"

"Naughty" she had not been, but — she felt her cheeks flush — look down she could not, as she said to herself that she was afraid she had been —

The word was taken out of her thoughts and expressed just as she came to it.

"Silly," said the clear soft voice. "Silly little Mavis. What is it all about? Is everything going wrong at the first trial?"

Then as Mavis gazed, the silvery-blue mist grew firmer and less vague, and gradually the lovely form and features became distinct.

"Oh dear princess," said the child, "I am *so* glad you have come. Yes, I dare say I am silly, but I am so unhappy;" and she poured out all her troubles. "I shall not be unhappy any more," she ended up, "now I know you are *true*. I had almost begun to fancy you were all a dream."

Forget-me-not smiled, but for a moment or two she did not speak. Then she said —

"What is it you are afraid of Ruby doing — Ruby and Bertrand?"

"Playing some unkind trick on Winfried," replied Mavis eagerly; "or even worse — for Ruby knows that would hurt him most — on his old grandfather. It would be so horrid, so *wicked*," and Mavis's voice grew tearful again, "when they have been so kind to us. Oh dear princess, will you stop them?"

Forget-me-not looked at her gravely.

"My child," she said, "do they not *know* it would be wrong to do such a thing?"

"Yes," Mavis replied, "of course they do."

"Then how could I stop them? I mean to say, what would be the good of stopping them, if they know already it is wrong?" said the princess.

Mavis looked puzzled.

"But if—if—they were to hurt or frighten old Adam or Winfried?" she said.

Forget-me-not smiled again.

"Ah yes," she said, "*that* I can promise you shall not be. But beyond that, if it is in their hearts wilfully to do what they know to be wrong, I fear, little Mavis, I fear they must do it, and perhaps learn thereby. When people *know*—"

Mavis's eyes told that she understood; she looked very grave, but still somewhat relieved.

"I am glad you won't let it hurt Winfried or his grandfather," she said. "But oh, I can't bear Ruby to be made naughty by that horrid boy," and she seemed on the point of bursting into tears. "Dear princess," she went on, "couldn't you speak to her—the way you do to me? You make me feel that I would—I would do *anything* you told me."

"Dear child, Ruby cannot hear me yet; she cannot see me. If she could, she would feel as you. Be patient, Mavis. Love her as you have always done; that will not be difficult. But that is not all. You must try to love Bertrand too."

Mavis's face grew very long.

"I don't think I *can*," she said at last.

"But you must, sooner or later, and it may as well be sooner. I will tell you one thing — a secret, which perhaps will make it easier for you. I mean to make him love *me* before I have done with him, though he may begin by hating me."

The little girl looked very grave.

"And Ruby?" she said. "I should care most for Ruby to love you."

Strange to say, Forget-me-not's eyes looked sadder than when she had been talking of Bertrand.

"It may be more difficult," she murmured, so low that Mavis hardly caught the words.

"Oh no, dear princess," she said eagerly, "Ruby isn't anything like as naughty as Bertrand. You mustn't fancy that. She's just — just — she doesn't think —"

"I know," said Forget-me-not; but that was all, and her eyes still looked sad.

Then she glanced round. The old room seemed like a background to her lovely figure, it was like gazing at a picture in a dark setting.

"I must go," she said, "and when I go you will be all in the dark. The clouds are so heavy and the day is getting on. Can you find your way all down the stair alone, Mavis? The others have not thought about leaving you up here alone."

"I don't think I mind," said Mavis; but her voice

was a little tremulous, for the corner where the door was, across the room from where Forget-me-not stood, loomed dark and gloomy.

The princess smiled.

" Yes you do, dear. Don't tell stories. I was only trying your courage a tiny bit. Come here, darling."

Mavis crept nearer her, nearer than she had yet been.

" I am afraid of soiling your lovely dress," she said. " My pinafore's rather dirty ; we've been playing all over the dusty rooms, you see."

Then Forget-me-not laughed. Her talking was charming, her smile was bewitching, her grave sad looks were like solemn music — what words have we left to describe her laugh? I can think of none. I can only tell you that it made little Mavis feel as if all the birds in the trees, all the flowers in the fields, all the brooks and waterfalls, all the happy joyous things in the world had suddenly come together with a shout — no, shout is too loud and rough, — with a warble and flutter of irrepressible glee.

" Oh," said Mavis, " how beautiful it is to hear you, princess, and how — "

She did not finish her sentence. In another moment she felt herself lifted up — up in the air ever so far, it seemed, and then cosily deposited most comfortably on Forget-me-not's shoulder. It was years and years since Mavis had thought herself small enough to ride even on her father's shoulder — great, strong, tall father — and the princess who looked so slight and fairy-like, how could she be so strong? Yet the arms that had lifted her *were* strong, strong and firm as father's, nay stronger. And the hand that held her up in her place was so secure in its gentle grasp that the little girl felt she *could* not fall, and that is a very pleasant feeling, I can assure you.

"Shut your eyes, Mavis," said Forget-me-not, "I am quick in my movements. You are quite firm — there now — I have thrown my scarf over you. I am going to take you rather a round-about way, I warn you."

A soft whirr and rush — where were they? Out of the window somehow they had got, for Mavis felt the chilly air and heard the swish of the rain, though strange to say the chill seemed only a pleasant freshness, and the raindrops did not touch her. Then up, up — dear, dear, where *were* they off to? Had Forget-me-not suddenly turned into the old woman who goes up to brush away the cobwebs in the sky? Mavis laughed as the fancy struck her; she did not care, not she, the higher the better, the faster they flew the merrier she felt. Till at last there came a halt. Forget-me-not stopped short with a long breath.

"Heigh-ho!" she exclaimed, "I've given you a toss up, haven't I? Look out, Mavis; we've come ever so far, — peep out and you'll see the stars getting ready to bid you good-evening. It's quite clear, of course, up here above the clouds."

Mavis opened her eyes and peeped out from the folds of Forget-me-not's scarf, which, light as it was, had yet a marvellous warmth about it.

Clear, I should think it *was* clear! Never had Mavis pictured to herself anything so beautiful as that evening sky, up "above the clouds," as the princess had said. I have never seen it, so I cannot very well describe it; indeed, I should be rather afraid to do so on hearsay, for I should be sure to make some mistake, and to name the wrong planets and constellations.

"Oh," said Mavis, "how nice!"

It was rather a stupid little word to say, but Forget-me-not was too "understanding" to mind.

"Look about you well for a minute or two. Who knows when you may have such a chance again?" and for a little there was silence. Then "Shut your eyes again, dear, and clasp me tight; little girls are apt to get giddy in such circumstances. Yes, that's right."

"The stars are like your eyes," said Mavis.

Then again the soft rush; a plunge downwards this time, which made Mavis need no second bidding to clasp her friend closely. There came over her a misty, sleepy feeling. She could not have told exactly when they stopped; she only felt a sort of butterfly kiss on her eyes, and a breath that sounded like good-night, and then — she was standing in the school-room by the fire; the lamp was lighted, it looked bright and cosy, and Mavis had never felt happier or stronger in her life.

"That nice fresh air has brightened me up so," she said to herself. But her hands were rather cold. She went close up to the fire to warm them. There was no one in the room.

"I wonder where Ruby and Bertrand are," thought Mavis. Just then she heard Miss Hortensia's voice.

"Poor dear," she was saying. "Ruby, how could you be so thoughtless? I must get lights at once and go and look for her."

"We've called and called up the stair, but she didn't answer," said Ruby in rather an ashamed tone of voice.

"Called," repeated Miss Hortensia, "why didn't you *go?*"

"It was so dark when we remembered about her, and — "

"You were afraid, I suppose," said her cousin. "Really; and yet you would leave poor Mavis all alone — and a great boy like you, Bertrand."

"*I* wasn't afraid, but I wasn't going to bother to go up all that way. She could come down by herself," said Master Bertrand rudely.

But before Miss Hortensia could reply again Mavis ran out.

"Here I am, dear cousin," she said. "I'm all right." And indeed she did look all right, as she stood there sideways in the doorway, the light from the room behind her falling on her pretty hair and fair face.

"The dear child," thought Miss Hortensia. "No one could say Mavis isn't as pretty as Ruby now." And aloud she exclaimed: "My darling, where have you been? And were you afraid up there in the dark all by yourself?"

"Why didn't you come with us?" said Ruby crossly. "It was all your own fault."

"I didn't mind," said Mavis. "I'm only sorry cousin Hortensia was frightened. I'm all right, you see."

"I was frightened about you too," grumbled Ruby.

"*I* wasn't," said Bertrand with a rough laugh. "There's nothing to *frighten* one up in that cockloft; dingy, misty place that it is."

"Misty!" exclaimed Miss Hortensia in surprise, "what does the child mean?"

"Bertrand will say the turret was full of blue smoke," said Ruby, "and that it hurt his eyes."

"It did," said the boy; "they're smarting still."

Mavis smiled. Miss Hortensia seemed perplexed, and rather anxious to change the subject.

"I do hope," she said, "that to-morrow will be fine, so that Bertrand and you, Ruby, may get rid of some of your spirits out-of-doors."

"I hope too that it will be fine," said Ruby meaningly. "Bertrand and I have planned a very long walk. You needn't come," she went on, turning to Mavis, "if you think you'd be tired."

"I don't get tired quicker than you do," said Mavis quietly. Her heart sank within her at Ruby's tone; for though she was glad to think Forget-me-not would prevent any harm to old Adam or Winfried, she did not like to think of Ruby's heartlessness and folly. And when she glanced at Bertrand and saw the half-scornful smile on his face, it was all she could do to keep back her tears.

All that evening the rain kept pouring down in torrents, and the wind beat on the window, shaking even the heavy frames, like a giant in a fury, determined to make his way in.

"What a storm," said Miss Hortensia more than once, with a little shiver. "I cannot bear to think of the poor souls at sea."

Bertrand laughed.

"It would be great fun to see a shipwreck, if one was safe out of harm's way. I wouldn't mind staying up in that musty old turret a whole afternoon to have a good view."

Even Ruby was startled.

"Oh Bertrand," she said, "you can't know what a shipwreck means if you speak like that."

"I've read stories of them," said the boy, "so I should know."

There was a very slight touch of something in his tone which made Mavis wonder if he really meant all the naughty things he said. She glanced up at him quickly.

"If there ever were a shipwreck here," she said, "I know who'd help and who wouldn't."

Bertrand's face hardened at once.

"That's meant for me,' he retorted; "for me and that precious lout of a friend of yours. You think him so grand and brave! Ah well! wait a bit and see. When people don't know their proper place they must be taught it."

Mavis drew herself up.

"Yes," she said, "we *will* wait a bit and see. But it won't be the sort of seeing you'll like perhaps."

"You've no business to speak like that," said Ruby. "I think you're quite out of your mind about that common boy and his grandfather — or else — and I shouldn't wonder if it was that, they've bewitched you, somehow."

She dropped her voice with the last words, for she did not want her cousin to hear. But Miss Hortensia. though she was busily counting the rows of her knitting at the other end of the room, noticed the tone of the children's voices.

"Come, come, my dears," she said, "no wrangling — it would be something quite new here. I do *hope*," she added to herself, "that it will be fine to-morrow; it is so much better for children when they can get out."

It *was* fine "to-morrow"; very fine. It was almost impossible for the little girls to believe that so few hours before the storm spirits had been indulging in their wild games, when they looked out of their window on to the bright clear wintry sky, where scarcely a cloud was to be seen, the sun smiling down coldly but calmly: not a breath of wind moving the great fir-trees on the south side of the castle. Yet looking a little closer there were some traces of the night's work; the ground was strewn with branches, and the last of the leaves had found their way down to their resting-place on old Mother Earth's brown lap.

In spite of her anxieties, Mavis could not help her spirits rising.

"What a nice afternoon Ruby and I might have had with Winfried, if *only* Bertrand hadn't come," she thought.

Ruby was all smiles and gaiety.

"Perhaps," Mavis went on to herself, "perhaps she's really going to be nice and good. And if we two keep together, we can stop Bertrand being very naughty."

Miss Hortensia was anxious for them to profit by the fine day. She had not much faith in the clear thin sunshine's lasting, she said, and she shortened the lessons so that dinner might be very early, and the afternoon free.

It was still very bright and fine when the three

children found themselves standing at the entrance of the archway, on the sea side of the castle.

"Which way shall we go?" said Mavis.

"Oh, down to the shore," Ruby replied. "We may," she went on, with a very slight glance in Bertrand's direction, and a tone in her voice which struck Mavis oddly, though she scarcely knew why —"we *may* meet Winfried."

"Yes," said Bertrand in an off-hand way. "I told the fellow we might be somewhere about if it was fine to-day, and I said he might as well have his boat ready. I don't mind paying him for the use of it. I've any amount of pocket-money;" and he thrust his hands into his pockets, jingling the coins which were in them.

Mavis thought to herself that she had never disliked him as much as now. But she said nothing, and they all three walked on. The pathway soon became steep and rugged, as I have told you. Ruby and Mavis were accustomed to it, and Bertrand was a strong, well-made boy. Still none of them were agile and nimble as the fisher-lad.

"You should see Winfried running down here," said Ruby; "he goes like a stag, or a chamois, rather."

She glanced at Bertrand as she spoke. Notwithstanding her alliance with him, there was something in Ruby's nature that made it impossible for her to resist vexing him by this little hit.

The black look came over the boy's face.

"What do you mean by that?" he muttered. "I'm not going to ——"

"Rubbish, Bertrand," interrupted Ruby. "I never said anything about *you*. Winfried's a fisher-boy; it's his business to scramble about."

Then she went close up to her cousin and whispered something to him, which seemed to smooth him down, though this only made Mavis more anxious and unhappy.

CHAPTER VIII.

A NAUGHTY PLAN.

" The boatie rows, the boatie rows, the boatie rows fu' weel."

EWEN.

THEY were nearly at the cove, when they caught sight of a scarlet cap moving up and down among the rocks.

"There's Winfried," cried Mavis joyfully. She could not help having a feeling of safety when the fisher-lad was with them, in spite of her fears about the mischief the other two were planning. " Winfried, Winfried," she called, " here we are."

He glanced up with his bright though rather mysterious smile.

" I knew you'd be coming," he said quietly.

" Of course you did," said Bertrand in his rough, rude way, " considering I told you to meet us here. Have you got that boat of yours ready ? "

" Yes," said Winfried, and he pointed towards the cove. There, sure enough, was the little boat, bright and dainty, the sun shining on its pretty cushions and on the white glistening oars.

Bertrand was running forward, when there came a sudden exclamation from Ruby. She had put up her hand to her neck.

106

"Oh, my cross," she cried, "my little silver cross. I forgot to fetch it from the turret-room. I left it there last night, and I meant to go and get it this morning. And I daren't go on the sea without it — I'd be drowned, I know I should be."

Mavis looked at her.

"Ruby," she said, "I don't think you could have left it up there. You had no reason to take it off up there."

"Oh, but I did, I did," said Ruby. "I have a trick of taking it off; the cord gets entangled in my hair. I know it's there."

"I'll fetch it you," said Bertrand, with perfectly astounding good-nature. And he actually set off up the rocky path. Winfried started forward.

"I will go," he said. "I can run much faster than he," and he hastened after Bertrand.

But Bertrand had exerted himself unusually. He was already some way up before Winfried overtook him.

"No," he said, when Winfried explained why he had come, "I want to go. But you may as well come too. I want to carry down my fishing-tackle — I'd forgotten it. You haven't got any in the boat, I suppose?"

"No," said Winfried, "it would keep us out too long. It's too cold for the little ladies, and we should have to go too far out to sea."

"I'll bring it all the same," said Bertrand doggedly; "so mind your own business." But as Winfried walked on beside him without speaking, he added more civilly, "you may as well look at it and tell me if it's the right kind. It's what my father gave me."

"I'm pretty sure it's not right," said Winfried. "The fishing here is quite different to anything you've ever seen. And anyway we cannot keep your cousins waiting while we look at it."

They were at the arched entrance by now.

"Well, then," said Bertrand, "you run up and look for the cross. No need for two of us to tire our legs. I'll wait here."

Winfried entered the castle, and after one or two wrong turnings found himself on the right stair. He knew pretty exactly where he had to go, for he had often looked up at the west turret from the outside. But just as he got to the door he was overtaken by Bertrand, who had naturally come straight up without any wrong turnings.

"What a time you've been," said Bertrand, pushing in before him. "Now, let's see — where did Ruby say she'd left her cross? Oh yes, hanging up there; she must have stood on a chair to reach it." And sure enough, on a nail pretty high up on the wall hung the little ornament.

Winfried drew forward a chair; in another minute he had reached down the cross.

"Here it is," he said, turning to Bertrand. But —

'Winfried drew forward a chair; in another minute he had reached down the cross.'   p. 108

he spoke to the air! Bertrand was gone. Winfried's face flushed; but he controlled himself. He walked quietly to the door and turned the handle. It did not open. It was locked from the outside. He was a prisoner!

"I knew something of the kind would come," he said to himself. "What will they do now? Poor little Mavis! I must trust her to the princess."

But he could not help a feeling of bitter anger. It was no light punishment to the active, energetic boy to have to spend all the bright afternoon hours shut up here like an old owl in a church tower. And he knew that till some one came to let him out, a prisoner he verily was. For he might have shouted his voice hoarse, no one down below could have heard him. And the chance of any one in the castle coming up was very small.

"What will gran think?" he said to himself. "And, if these naughty children try to play him any trick. I know Ruby more than half believes all that nonsense about his being a wizard and about the mermaids, and Bertrand will egg her on."

He went to the window and stood looking out, trying to keep down the dreadful restless *caged* feeling which began to come over him.

"How can I bear it?" he said. "If I had tools now, and could pick the lock: but some of these old locks are very strong, and I have nothing. If only I had wings;" and he gazed again out of the window.

When he turned round, though it was quite bright
and sunny outside, it almost seemed as if the evening
haze had somehow got into the room before its time.
It was filled with a thin bluish mist. Winfried's
eyes brightened.

" My princess!" he exclaimed. " Are you there?"

A little laugh answered him, and gradually the
mist drew together and into shape, and Forget-me-
not stood before him.

" My boy," she exclaimed. " I am surprised at you.
Why, you were looking quite depressed!"

Winfried reddened.

" It was the horrid feeling of being locked up," he
said. " I never felt it before, and — it seems such a
shame, such a mean trick. I wouldn't have minded
a stand-up fight with any fellow, but — "

" Of course you wouldn't; but you've got a good
bit farther than *that*, I hope, Winfried," she said with
a smile. " And besides, Bertrand is much smaller
than you. And it had to be, you know. I have explained enough to you — you and little Mavis : — it
had to be."

Winfried started.

" That's another thing," he said. " I am uneasy
about her. What will they do? They don't understand the boat, you know, princess, and she is alone
with them."

Forget-me-not smiled again.

" How faithless you are to-day, Winfried," she

said. "Mavis will be getting before you if you don't take care, simple and ignorant as she is. Can't you trust her to me?" And as the boy's face brightened, "Come," she said, "I see you are recovering your usual ground, so I will tell you how I am going to do. But first, shut your eyes, Winfried; and here, wrap the end of my scarf round you. You might feel giddy still, though it's not the first time. Ready?—that's right—there now, give me your hand—we're up on the window ledge. You were wishing for wings—isn't this as good as wings?"

*   *   *   *   *   *   *   *

Bertrand rushed down—as much as he could rush, that is to say, over the steep and rough path—to the shore where the sisters were waiting.

"Have you got it?" asked Mavis eagerly.

"What?" asked Bertrand, out of breath.

"*What?* Why, Ruby's cross, of course, that you went for. And where is Winfried?"

"All right," said Bertrand, in a curious voice; "he's coming directly. We're to get into the boat and go on a little way, keeping near the shore. He's coming down another way."

(Yes, Bertrand, that he is!)

Mavis looked up anxiously.

"And the cross?" she said.

"Winfried's got it," he said. Which was true. Then he turned away, the fact being that he was so choking with laughter that he was afraid of betraying himself.

"Ruby," he called, "come and help me to drag the boat a little nearer;" and as Ruby came close he whispered to her, "I've done it — splendidly — he's shut up in his tower! Locked in, and the locks are good strong ones — now we can have a jolly good spree without that prig of a fellow Only don't let Mavis know till we're safe out in the boat."

Ruby jumped with pleasure.

"What fun!" she exclaimed. "How capital! You have been clever, Bertrand. But take care, or Mavis will suspect something. Quick, Mavis," she went on, turning to her sister, "help us to pull in the boat. There, we can jump in now, Bertrand. You and Mavis steady it while I spring;" and in another moment she was in the boat, where her sister and Bertrand soon followed her.

All seemed well: the sky was clear and bright, the sun still shining. The faces of two of the party were sparkling with glee and triumph. But Mavis looked frightened and dissatisfied.

"I wish Winfried had come back with you, Bertrand," she said. "Why didn't he? Did cousin Hortensia keep him for anything?"

"Goodness, no," said Bertrand. "What a fuss you make, child! He's all right; you can look out for him, and tell me if you see him coming. I shall have enough to do with rowing you two."

"Winfried doesn't find the boat hard to row," said Mavis; "it's your own fault if it is hard. You might as well wait for him; he'd see us as he comes down the cliffs."

"Oh no, that would be nonsense," said Ruby hastily; "besides, he's not coming that way. You heard Bertrand say so. _I_ could row too, Bertrand," she went on.

But the boy had already got his oars in motion, and though he was neither skilful nor experienced, strange to say the little boat glided on with the utmost ease and smoothness.

"There now," said Bertrand, considerably surprised, to tell the truth, at his own success, "didn't I tell you I could row?"

"No," said Mavis bluntly, "you said just this moment you'd have enough to do to manage it."

"Mavis, why are you so cross?" said Ruby. "It is such a pity to spoil everything."

She spoke very smoothly and almost coaxingly, but Mavis looked her straight in the eyes, and Ruby grew uncomfortable and turned away. But just then a new misgiving struck Mavis.

"Bertrand," she cried, "either you can't manage the boat, or you're doing it on purpose. You're not keeping near the shore as you said you would. You're going right out to sea;" and she jumped up as if she would have snatched the oars from him.

"Sit down, Mavis," said Ruby. "I'm sure you know you should never jump about in a boat. It's all right. Don't you know there's — there's a current hereabouts?"

Current or no, *something* there was, besides Bertrand's rowing, that was rapidly carrying them away farther and farther from the shore. Mavis looked at Bertrand, not sure whether he could help himself or not. But—

"Winfried wouldn't have told you to keep near the shore if you couldn't," she said; "he knows all about the currents."

Bertrand turned with a rude laugh.

"Does he indeed?" he said. "It's more than I do; but all the same this current, or whatever it is that is taking us out so fast, has come just at the right minute. I never meant to keep near in, there's no fun in that. We're going a jolly good way out, and when we're tired of it we'll come back and land close to the old wizard's cottage. Ruby and I are going to play him a trick; we want to catch him with the mermaids Ruby heard singing the other day. If we set the villagers on him, they'll soon make an end of him and his precious grandson."

"Yes," said Ruby spitefully; "and a good riddance they'd be. That Winfried setting himself up over us all."

Mavis grew pale.

"Ruby; Bertrand," she said, "you cannot mean to be so wicked. You know the villagers are already set against old Adam rather, even though he has been so good to them, and if you stir them up—they might kill him if they really thought he was a wizard."

"We're not going to do anything till we know for ourselves," said Ruby. "We're first going to the cottage really to find out if it's true. You know yourself, Mavis, we *did* hear some one singing and speaking there the other day who wasn't to be seen when we got there. And I believe it *was* a mermaid, or — or a syren, or some witchy sort of creature."

Mavis was silent. She had her own thoughts about the voice they had overheard, thoughts which she could not share with the others.

"Oh, dear Princess Forget-me-not," she said to herself, "why don't you make them see you, and understand how naughty they are?"

For the moment she had forgotten the princess's promise that neither Winfried nor his grandfather should suffer any harm, and she felt terribly frightened and unhappy.

"Where is Winfried?" she said at last. "He will see us going out to sea when he comes down to the shore, and if he tells cousin Hortensia she can easily get some of the fishermen to come after us. They can row far quicker than you."

Bertrand stopped rowing to laugh more rudely than before.

"*Can* they?" he said. "I doubt it. And as for Winfried telling — why, he doesn't know; he's locked in safe and sound in the west turret! He'll be quite comfortable there for as long as I choose to leave him, and however he shouts no one can hear him.

Not that there's much fear of any of those lumbering boats overtaking us if they tried — why — "

He took up the oars again as he spoke, but before he began to row he half started and glanced round. No wonder; the boat was gliding out to sea without his help, quite as fast as when he was rowing.

" How — how it drifts ! " he said in a rather queer tone of voice. " Is there a current hereabouts, Ruby?"

" I suppose so," said Ruby. " Try and row the other way, that'll soon show you."

But it was all very well to speak of " trying." No efforts of Bertrand's had the very slightest effect on the boat. On it sped, faster and faster, as if laughing at him, dancing along the water as if it were alive and enjoying the joke. Bertrand grew angry, then, by degrees, frightened.

" It isn't my fault," he said. " I don't pretend to know all about the currents and tides and nonsense. You shouldn't have let me come out here, Ruby."

Ruby was terrified, but angry too.

" It isn't *my* fault," she said. " You planned it all; you know you did. And if we're all — "

" Be quiet, Ruby," said Mavis, who alone of the three was perfectly calm and composed. " If it stops you and Bertrand carrying out your naughty plan, I am very glad if we are taken out to sea."

" That's *too* bad of you," said Ruby, angry in spite of her terror. " I believe you'd rather we were drowned than that your precious Winfried and his grandfather should get what they deserve. And we *are* going to be drowned, or anyway starved to death. We're going faster and faster. Oh, I do believe there must be a whirlpool somewhere near here, and that we are going to be sucked into it."

She began to sob and cry. Bertrand, to do him justice, put a good face upon it. He looked pale but determined.

"This is what comes of having to do with people like that," he said vindictively. "I believe he's bewitched the boat to spite us. I'll have another try. however."

But it was all no use. The boat, slight and fragile as it seemed, resisted his efforts as if it were a living thing opposing him. Crimson with heat and vexation, the boy muttered some words, which it was to be hoped the girls did not catch. and flung down the oars in a rage. One fell inside. the other was just slipping over the edge when Mavis caught it. Strange to say, no sooner was it in her hold than the motion stopped; the boat lay still and passive on the water, swaying gently as if waiting for orders.

"We've got out of the current," exclaimed Ruby. "Try. Mavis, can you turn it?"

It hardly seemed to need trying. The boat turned almost. as it were, of itself, and in another moment they were quietly moving towards the shore. Nor did it seem to make any difference when Bertrand took the oars from Mavis and resumed his rowing.

"If I only waited another moment," he said. "We got out of the current just as you caught the oar, Mavis."

She shook her head doubtfully.

"I don't know. I don't think it was that," she said. "But anyway now it is all right again, and we are going back, you and Bertrand, Ruby, will not think of playing any trick, or setting the villagers on to old Adam."

"Why not, pray?" said Bertrand. "And—"

"I don't see what has made any difference," said Ruby pertly. "Suppose the horrid things had bewitched the boat, is that any reason for not showing them up? You think it's all your wonderful cleverness that got the boat round, do you, Mavis?"

"No, I don't. I think a good many things I'm not going to tell you," said the little girl. "But one thing I will tell you, *I* will not leave the boat or come on shore unless you promise me to give up your naughty cruel plan."

She spoke so firmly that Ruby was startled. And indeed her own words seemed to surprise Mavis herself. It was as if some one were whispering to her what to say. But on Bertrand they made no impression.

"You won't, won't you?" he said. "Ah, well. we'll see to that."

They were close to the shore by this time. The marvellous boat had "got over the ground," I was going to say — I mean the *water* — even more quickly than when going out to sea. And in another minute, thanks to something — no doubt Bertrand thought it was thanks to his wonderful skill — they glided quietly into the little landing-place where Winfried had brought them two days ago.

Up jumped Ruby.

"That's capital," she said. "We can easily make our way to the old wizard's cottage from here. And before we peep in on him himself, Bertrand, we may as well look round his garden, as he calls it. It is the queerest place you ever saw, full of caves and grottoes."

Both Bertrand and she had jumped on shore.

"Come on, Mavis," cried they. "What are you so slow about?"

For Mavis sat perfectly still in her place.

"I am not coming on shore," she said quietly, "not unless you promise to give up whatever mischief it is that you are planning."

"Nonsense," said Bertrand. "You just *shall* come: tell her she must. Ruby, you're the eldest."

"Come, Mavis," said Ruby. "You'd better come, for everybody's sake, I can tell you," she added meaningly. "If you're there you can look after your precious old wizard. I won't promise anything."

"No," Mavis repeated. "I will not come. We have no right to go forcing ourselves into his cottage. It is as much his as the castle is ours, and you know you have locked up Winfried on purpose so that he can't get out. No, I will not go with you."

"Then stay," shouted Bertrand, "and take the consequences."

And he dragged Ruby back from the boat.

CHAPTER IX.

BEGINNINGS?

CHILD WORLD.

"LET's run on fast a little way," said Bertrand, "to make her think we won't wait for her. That will frighten her, and she will run after us, you'll see. Don't look round, Ruby."

In his heart he really did not believe that Mavis would change her mind or run after them. And he did not care. Indeed, he much preferred having Ruby alone, as he knew he could far more easily persuade her by herself to join in his mischievous schemes. But he felt that she was half-hearted about leaving her sister, and so he did not hesitate to trick her too.

They hurried on for some distance. Then Ruby, who was growing both tired and cross, pulled her hand away from Bertrand.

"Stop," she said. "I'm quite out of breath. And I want to see if Mavis is coming."

Bertrand had to give in. They were on higher ground than the shore, and could see it clearly. There lay the little boat as they had left it, and

Mavis sitting in it calmly. To all appearance at least.

"She's not coming — not a bit of her," exclaimed Ruby angrily. "I don't believe you thought she would, Bertrand."

"She *will* come, you'll see," said the boy, "and even if she doesn't, what does it matter? We'll run on and spy out the old wizard and have some fun. Mavis will stay there safe enough till we get back."

"I thought you meant to go home by the village and tell the people about old Adam, if we *do* see anything queer," said Ruby.

"So I did, but if you're in such a fidget about Mavis perhaps we'd better go home as we came, and not say anything in the village to-day. I'd like to see what Master Winfried has been up to when we get back. Perhaps he'll have got some old witch to lend him a broomstick, and we shall find him flown;" and Bertrand laughed scornfully.

Ruby laughed too.

"I don't think that's likely," she said. "But there's no telling. I do wish he and his grandfather were out of the country altogether. There's something about Winfried that makes me feel furious. He *is* such a prig; and he's even got cousin Hortensia to think him a piece of perfection."

"He may take his perfections elsewhere, and he shall, too," said Bertrand. And the fierceness of his tone almost startled even Ruby.

They were not far from the old fisherman's cottage by this time. They stopped again to take breath. Mavis and the boat were not visible from where they stood, for the path went in and out among the rocks, and just here some large projecting boulders hid the shore from sight.

Suddenly, as if it came from some cave beneath their feet, both children grew conscious of a faint sound as of distant music. And every moment it became clearer and louder even though muffled. Bertrand and Ruby looked at each other.

" Mermaids!" both exclaimed.

" They always sing," said Bertrand.

" Yes," added Ruby, with her old confusion of ideas about syrens; "and they make people go after them by their singing, and then they catch them and kill them, and I'm not sure but what they *eat* them. I know I've read something about bare dry bones being found. Shall we put our fingers in our ears, Bertrand?" She looked quite pale with fear.

" Nonsense," said the boy. " That's only sailors at sea. They lure them in among the rocks. We're quite safe on dry land. Besides, I don't think it's *mermaids* that do that. They're miserable crying creatures; but *I* don't think they kill people."

The subterraneous music came nearer and nearer. Somehow the children could not *help* listening.

" Didn't you say you and Mavis heard singing the day you were here before — at the wizard's cottage, I mean?" said Bertrand.

"N-no, not exactly singing. It was laughing, and a voice calling out good-bye in a singing way," answered Ruby.

As if in response to her words, the singing suddenly stopped, and from below their feet — precisely below it seemed — came the sound of ringing, silvery laughter, clear and unmistakable.

"Oh," cried Ruby, "come away, Bertrand. I'm sure it's the mermaids, and they *will* catch us and kill us, you'll see."

Her boasted courage had not come to much. And yet there was nothing very alarming in the pretty sounds they had heard.

" And what if it is the mermaids? " said Bertrand coolly. "We came out to catch them, didn't we? It's just what we wanted. Come along, Ruby. How do we get to the cottage? There seems to be a sort of wall in front."

"We go round by the back," said Ruby. "It's there there are the queer grottoes and little caves. But you won't go far into them, will you, Bertrand? For I am not at all sure but that the mermaids come up from the sea through these caves ; you see they *do* come some underground way."

Bertrand gave a sort of grunt. What Ruby said only made him the more determined to explore as far as he possibly could.

They entered the strange little garden I have already described without further adventure. There seemed no one about, no sound of any kind broke the almost unnatural stillness.

"How *very* quiet it is," said Ruby with a little shiver. "And there's no smoke coming out of the chimney — there was the last time, for there was a good fire in the kitchen where old Adam was."

And as she said this there came over her the remembrance of the kind old man's gentle hospitality and interest in them. Why had she taken such a hatred to Winfried and his grandfather, especially since Bertrand's arrival? She could not have given any real reason.

"I hope he isn't very ill — or — *dead*," she said, dropping her voice. "And Winfried locked up and not able to get to him. It would be our fault, Bertrand."

"Nonsense," said Bertrand roughly, with his usual scornful contempt of any softer feelings. "He's fallen asleep over his pipe and glass of grog. I dare say he drinks lots of grog — those fellows always do."

"I'm sure *he* doesn't," contradicted Ruby, feeling angry with herself as well as Bertrand. "Let's go to the window and peep in before we look at the caves."

She ran round to the front, followed by her cousin, taking care to make as little sound as possible. She remembered on which side of the door was the kitchen, and softly approached what she knew must be its window. But how surprised she was when she looked in! It was the kitchen; she remembered the shape of the room; she recognised the neat little fireplace, but all was completely deserted. Every trace of furniture had disappeared; old Adam's large chair by the hearth might never have been in existence, well as she remembered it. Except that it was clean and swept, the room might not have been inhabited for years.

Ruby turned to Bertrand, who was staring in at another window.

"I say, Ruby," he whispered, "the room over here is quite — "

"I know," she said. "So is the kitchen. They're gone, Bertrand, quite gone, and we've had all our trouble for nothing. It's too bad."

"*They*," repeated Bertrand. "you can't say *they*, when you know that Winfried is locked up in the turret-room."

"Oh," exclaimed Ruby starting. "I quite forgot. He must have hidden his grandfather somewhere. And yet I don't see how they could have managed it so quietly. We always know when any of the village people are moving their furniture; they send to borrow our carts."

"Well,' said Bertrand, "there's one thing certain. If you didn't believe it before, you must now; I should think even Mavis would — the old fellow *is* a wizard, and so's his precious grandson."

"Shall we go into the house?" said Ruby, though she looked half afraid to do so.

"Isn't the door locked?" said Bertrand, trying it as he spoke. It yielded to his touch; he went in, followed, though tremblingly, by Ruby.

But after all there was little or nothing to see: the three rooms, though scrupulously clean, even the windows shining bright and polished, were perfectly empty. As the children strolled back to the kitchen, annoyed and disappointed, feeling, to tell the truth, rather small, something caught Ruby's eye in one corner of the room. It was a small object, gleaming bright and blue on the white stones of the floor. She ran forward and picked it up, it was a tiny bunch of forget-me-nots tied with a scrap of ribbon; the same large brilliant kind of forget-me-not as those which she and Mavis had so admired on their first visit to the now deserted cottage. She gave a little cry.

"Look, Bertrand," she said, "they can't have been long gone. These flowers are quite fresh. I wonder where they came from. They must have been growing in a pot in the house, for there are none in the garden. I looked as we came through."

Bertrand glanced at the flowers carelessly.

"Wizards," he began, "can —"

But his sentence was never finished. For as he spoke there came a sudden gust of wind down the wide chimney, so loud and furious that it was as startling as a clap of thunder. Then it subsided again, but for a moment or two a long low wail sounded overhead, gradually dying away in the distance.

"What was that?" said Bertrand. While the sounds lasted both children had stood perfectly still.

"The wind of course," said Ruby. She was more accustomed than her cousin to the unexpected vagaries of the storm spirits so near the sea, still even she seemed startled. "It's often like that," she was beginning to say, but she hesitated. "It *was* very loud," she added.

"There must be rough weather coming," said Bertrand. "We'd better go home by the road, I think, Ruby."

"*We*," exclaimed Ruby indignantly. "Do you mean you and me, Bertrand? And what about Mavis?"

"She can come on shore," replied the boy carelessly. "She knows where we are. It's her own fault. Come along, there's nothing to wait for in this empty old hole. I want you to show me the caves outside."

"I'll try to signal to Mavis first," said Ruby. "I'll tie my handkerchief to a stick and wave it about. She can see us up here quite well, and perhaps when she finds we're alone she'll come."

They left the cottage, and Ruby got out her handkerchief. But it was small use. For just as they stepped on to the rough little terrace in front from whence they could clearly see the shore, there came

'—Bertrand—look—where is Mavis —Mavis and the boat; can you see them?'

P. 129

another and even — it seemed so at least now they were standing outside — more violent blast. It was all Ruby could do to keep her feet, and when she recovered from the giddying effect of the wind she was still breathless and shaken. And that the hurricane was gathering strength every second was plain to be seen; the waves were dashing in excitedly, the sky at one side had that strange lurid purple colour which foretells great disturbance.

But it was not these things only which made Ruby turn pale and shiver.

"Bertrand," she gasped, "I don't know if there's something the matter with my eyes, I can't see clearly — Bertrand — look — where is Mavis — Mavis and the boat; can you see them?"

Bertrand shaded his brow with his hand and gazed.

"'Pon my soul," he said, "it's very odd. *I* can't see them. And there's not been time for Mavis to have rowed out to sea or even to have drifted out; we can see right out ever so far, and there's no boat; not a sign of one."

"Can — can she have landed and dragged the boat ashore somehow?" said Ruby, her teeth chattering with cold and fear.

"No," said Bertrand, "we'd certainly see her and the boat in that case."

"Then, where is she?" cried Ruby. "*Bertrand,* you must care. What do you think has become of her?"

"Can't say, I'm sure," said the boy. "The boat may have capsized: the sea's awfully rough now."

"Do you mean that Mavis may be drowned or drowning?" screamed Ruby. She had to scream, even had she been less terribly excited, for the roar of wind was on them again, and her voice was scarcely audible.

"I don't see that she need be drowned," said Bertrand. "It's shallow. She *may* have crept on shore, and be lying somewhere among those big stones; and if not, can't your precious wizard friends look after her? She's fond enough of them."

He was partly in earnest; but Ruby took it all as cruel heartless mocking. She turned upon him furiously.

"You're a brutal wicked boy," she screamed. "I wish you were drowned; I wish you had never come near us; I wish — " she stopped, choked by her fury and misery, and by the wind which came tearing round again.

Bertrand came close to her.

"As you're so busy wishing," he called into her ear, "you'd better wish you hadn't done what you have done yourself. It was all you who started the plan, and settled how we were to trick Winfried into the turret-room; you know you did."

"And did I plan to drown Mavis, my own darling little sister?" returned Ruby as well as she could speak between her sobs and breathlessness. "Come down to the shore with me this moment and help me to look for her, if you're not altogether a cruel heartless bully."

"Not I," said Bertrand, "we'd probably get drowned ourselves. Just see how the waves come leaping in; they look as if they were alive. I believe it's all witches' work together. I'm not going to trust myself down there. Come and show me the grottoes and the caves, Ruby. We may as well shelter in them till the wind goes down a bit. We can't do Mavis any good; if she's on the shore she can take care of herself, and if she's under the water *we* can't reach her;" and he caught hold of Ruby to pull her along, but she tore herself from his grasp with a wrench.

"You wicked, you heartless, brutal boy," she cried. "I don't care if I am drowned; I would rather be drowned with Mavis than stay alive with you."

And almost before Bertrand knew what she was doing, Ruby was rushing through the little garden at the back of the cottage on her way to descend the rough path to the shore.

He stood looking after her coolly for a moment or two with his hands in his pockets. He tried to whistle, but it was not very successful; the wind had the best of it.

"I don't believe Mavis has come to any harm," he said aloud, though speaking to himself, and almost as if trying to excuse his own conduct. "Anyway, I don't see that it's my business to look after her, it was all her own obstinacy."

He kicked roughly at the pebbles at his feet, and as he did so, his glance fell on a tiny speck of colour just where he was kicking. It was one of the blue flowers Ruby had found in the cottage. Bertrand stooped and picked it up, and, strange to say, he handled it gently. But as he looked at it there came again to him the queer smarting pain in his eyes which he had complained of in the turret-room, and glancing up he became aware that the wind had suddenly gone down, everything had become almost unnaturally still, while a thin bluish haze seemed gathering closely round where he stood. Bertrand rubbed his eyes.

"There can't be smoke here," he said. "What can be the matter with my eyes?" and he rubbed them impatiently. It did no good.

"No, that will do no good," said a voice. It seemed quite near him.

"Look up;" and in spite of himself the boy could not help looking up.

"*Oh*," he screamed; "*oh*, what is it? what is it?"

For an agony, short but indescribable, had darted through his eyeballs, piercing, it seemed to him, to his very brain; and Bertrand was not in some ways a cowardly boy.

There was silence. perfect, dead silence, and gradually the intense aching, which the short terrible pain had left, began to subside. As it did so, and Bertrand ventured to look up again, he saw that — what he had seen, he could not describe it better — was gone, the haze had disappeared, the air was again clear, but far from still, for round the corner of the old cottage the blast now came rushing and tearing, as if infuriated at having been for a moment obliged to keep back ; and with it now came the rain, such rain as the inland-bred boy had never seen before — blinding, drenching, lashing rain, whose drops seemed to cut and sting, with such force did they fall. It added to his confusion and bewilderment. Like a hunted animal he turned and ran, anywhere to get shelter; and soon he found himself behind the house, and then the thought of the grottoes the little girls had told him of returned to his mind.

"I won't go back into that witches' hole," he said to himself as he glanced back at the house. "I'll shelter in one of the grottoes."

As he thought this he caught sight of an opening in the rockery before him. It was the entrance to the very cave where Mavis had been left by Ruby. Bertrand ran in : what happened to him there you shall hear in good time.

CHAPTER X.

"FORGET-ME-NOT LAND."

"A world . . .
Where the month is always June."

THREE WORLDS.

RUBY meanwhile was running or rather stumbling down the stones. She cried and sobbed as she went; her pretty face had never, I think, looked so woebegone and forlorn; for it was new to her to be really distressed or anxious about anything.

"Mavis, Mavis," she called out every now and then, "are you there, darling? can't you answer?" as if, even had the wind been less wildly raging, Mavis could possibly have heard her so far off.

And before long Ruby was obliged to stop for a moment to gather strength and breath. The wind seemed to increase every minute. She turned her back to it for a second; the relief was immense; and just then she noticed that she was still clutching the little bunch of flowers she had picked up. They made her begin to cry again.

"Mavis loves them so," she thought, and her memory went back to the happy peaceful afternoon they had spent with old Adam and his grandson. How kind they were, and how nice the cakes were that Winfried had made for them himself!

"Oh," thought Ruby, "I wish Bertrand had never come! It's all —" but there she hesitated. There had been truth in her cousin's mean reproach, that the mischief and the cruel tricks they had planned had been first thought of by *her*. And Ruby knew, too, in her heart, that she had not been gentle or unselfish or kind long before she had ever seen Bertrand. She had not been so actively naughty because she had had no chance of being so, as it were. The coming together of the two selfish, unfeeling natures had been like the meeting of the flint and steel, setting loose the hidden fire.

And besides this, for Bertrand there might have been some excuse; he had been neglected and yet spoilt; he had never known what it was truly to love any one, whereas Ruby had lived in love all her life; and this was her return for it.

"I have killed my little Mavis," she sobbed. "Yes, it has been all me. We needn't have minded Bertrand; he couldn't have made me naughty if I hadn't let him. Oh, Mavis, Mavis, whatever shall I do?"

Her glance fell again on the flowers in her hand. They were not the least withered or spoilt, but as fresh as if just newly gathered. They seemed to smile up at her, and she felt somehow comforted.

"Dear little flowers," she said. Seldom in her life

had Ruby spoken so tenderly. She started, as close beside her she heard a faint sigh.

"Ruby," said a voice, "can you hear me?"

"Yes," said the little girl, beginning to tremble.

"But you cannot see me? and yet I am here, close to you, as I have often been before. Try Ruby, try to see me."

"Are — are you a mermaid, or a — that other thing?" asked the child.

There came a little laugh, scarcely a laugh, then the sigh again.

"If you could see me you would know how foolish you are," said the voice. "But I must have patience — it will come — your eyes are not strong, Ruby; they are not even as strong as Bertrand's."

"Yes. they are," said Ruby indignantly. "I've never had sore eyes in my life, and Bertrand's have hurt him several times lately."

"I know: so much the better for him," was the reply. "Well, good-bye for the present, Ruby. Go on to look for Mavis; you must face it all — there, the rain is coming now. Ah!"

And with this, which sounded like a long sigh, the voice seemed to waft itself away, and down came the rain. The same swirl which had been too much for sturdy Bertrand was upon Ruby now, standing, too, in a far more exposed place. with no shelter near, and the rough rocky path before her. She did not stand long; she turned again and began to descend, stumbling, slipping, blinded by the rain, dashed and knocked about by the wind.

"She might have helped me, whoever she was that spoke to me," sobbed Ruby. "It isn't my fault if I can't see creatures like that. I'm not good enough, I suppose."

As she said these last words, or thought them, rather, a queer little thrill passed through her, and something, in spite of herself, make her look up. Was it — no, it could not be — she had suddenly thought a gleam of sunshine and blue sky had flashed on her sight; but no, the storm was too furious. "Yet still, I did," thought Ruby, "I did see something bright and blue, as if two of my little flowers had got up there and were looking down on me."

She glanced at her hand; the forget-me-nots were gone!

"I must have dropped them," she said. "Oh dear, dear!"

And yet as she struggled on again she did not feel *quite* so miserable.

Yet it was terribly hard work, and every moment her anxiety about Mavis increased; Ruby had never *felt* so much in all her life.

"Who could it be that spoke to me so strangely?" she asked herself over and over again. "And what can I do to be able to see her? I wonder if Mavis has seen her, I wonder —" and suddenly there came into her mind the remembrance of Miss Hortensia's long-ago story of the vision in the west turret.

"There was something about forget-me-nots in it," she thought dreamily. "Could it have been true?"

How she had mocked at the story!

She had at last reached the shore by this time. The rain still fell in pitiless torrents, but the wind had fallen a little, and down here she seemed rather less exposed than on the face of the cliffs. Still Ruby was completely drenched through: never before had she had any conception of the misery to which some of our poor fellow-creatures are exposed to almost every day of their lives. And yet, her fears for Mavis overmastered all her other sufferings: for the first time Ruby thought of another more than of herself.

"Mavis, dear little Mavis, Mavis darling, where are you?" she sobbed wildly, her teeth chattering, while terrible shivers shook her from head to foot. "Oh, it *can't* be that she is under those dreadful, fierce, leaping waves. They look as if they were dancing in cruel joy over something they had got;" and a shudder worse than those caused by the cold went through the poor child.

"Mavis," she called out at last, after she had peered round about every large stone, every corner where her sister could possibly have tried to find shelter, without coming upon the slightest trace of either the child or the boat, "you must be in the sea.

I'll go after you; it doesn't matter if I am drowned if you are. Perhaps — perhaps the mermaids are keeping you safe; there are kind ones among them it says in the fairy stories."

And she turned resolutely to the water. It was cold, icily cold as it touched first her feet, then her ankles, then crept up to her knees; it seemed to catch her breath even before it was at all deep. Ruby felt her powers going and her senses failing.

"I shall never be able to find Mavis even if she is under the sea," she thought to herself, just as a huge wave caught her in its rolling clutch, and she knew no more.

It seemed as if time beyond counting, years, centuries had passed when Ruby came to her senses again, enough to know that she was herself, gradually to remember that once, long ago, there had been a little girl called Ruby, somewhere, somehow, and that some one dear, most dear to her, had been in awful danger from which she had tried to rescue her. And through all the long mist, through all the dream wanderings of her spirit, in which maybe it had been learning lessons, the fruit of which remained, though the teachings themselves were forgotten, — for who knows, who can limit what we *do* learn in these mysterious ways? Ruby's guardian angel must have rejoiced to see that the thought of her sister, not herself, was uppermost.

"Mavis," was the first word she whispered;

"Mavis, are you alive? Are you not drowned, darling? But it was such a *very* long time ago. Perhaps the world is finished. But Mavis — I thought Mavis was dead; and, oh! who are you?" she ended with a thrill which seemed to make her quite alive and awake. "Are you the fairy in the turret? And what are you doing to my eyes?"

She sat up and rubbed them. There was the strangest feeling in them — not pain now; indeed it was, though strange, a beautiful feeling. They felt drawn upwards, upwards to something or some one, and a new light and strength seemed to fill them, light and strength and colour such as Ruby had never before even *imagined*. And the some one — yes, it was the lovely gracious figure, with the exquisite never-, once seen, to-be-forgotten eyes, of Winfried's princess. Ruby saw her at last!

A smile overspread the sweet face; the blue eyes shone with gladness.

"How often I have hoped for this," she murmured. "No, Ruby, you will never know how often. Darling, shut your eyes, you must not strain them; shut your eyes and think of Mavis, and trust yourself to me."

Ruby obeyed; she had not even looked round to see where she was; she only felt that she was lying on something soft and warm and *dry*; oh, how nice it was to feel dry again. For now the distant, long-ago sensation began to fade, and she remembered everything clearly as if it had happened, say, yesterday or the day before at farthest. The naughty mischief she and Bertrand had been planning, the strange little boat, the deserted cottage, the hurricane, and the misery about Mavis, the plunge in search of her into the sea, even to the loss of the forget-me-nots, which had been her only comfort, all came back: and with it a wonderful delightful feeling of hope and peace and trust, such as she had never known before. She gave herself up to the kind strong arms that clasped her round. "She will take me to Mavis," she thought; "and oh, I *will* try never, never to be selfish and unkind and naughty again."

Then, still wrapped in the soft warm mantle or rug she had felt herself lying upon, she was lifted upwards, upwards still, she knew not and cared not whither, for Ruby's eyes were closed and she was fast asleep, and this time her sleep was dreamless.

"Ruby, my own little Ruby," were the first words she heard. They awoke her as nothing else would have done.

"Mavis," she whispered.

Yes, it was Mavis. She was leaning over the couch on which Ruby lay. Never had Ruby seen her so bright and sweet and happy-looking.

"Mavis," Ruby repeated. "And you weren't drowned, darling? At least;" and as she raised herself a little she looked round her doubtfully, "at least, not unless this is heaven? It looks like it—

only," with a deep sigh, "it can't be, for if it were, *I* shouldn't be in it."

"No, darling, it isn't heaven, but it's a beautiful place, and I *think* it must be a little on the way there. It's one of the homes of our princess; she won't tell me the name, but I call it Forget-me-not Land. Isn't that a good name? Look all about, Ruby."

They were in a little arbour, in one corner of what one would have called a garden, except that gardens are usually enclosed. They don't stretch as far as the eyes can see, which was the case here. A soft clear yet not dazzling or glaring light was over everything, yet there was no sun visible in the sky. And as Ruby gazed and gazed she began to feel that there were differences between this garden and any others she had ever seen. One of these Mavis pointed out to her.

"Do you see, Ruby," she said, "that all the flowers in this garden are our wild flowers, though they are such beauties?" She stooped to gather one or two blossoms growing close beside her as she spoke. "See, here are the same kind of forget-me-nots that were at the old cottage, and that we found so strangely on the castle terrace. And here are violets and primroses and snowdrops, all the spring flowers; and the summer ones too, honeysuckle and dog-roses; and even the tiny common ones, buttercups and daisies, and celandine and pimpernel, and eye-bright and shepherd's-purse, and — and — "

"But you're mixing them all up together," said Ruby. "They don't all come at the same time of year."

"Yes, they do *here*," said Mavis. "That's the wonder. I found it out for myself almost immediately, and the princess was so pleased I did. I think this garden is a sort of nursery for wild flowers; you see up where we live there are no gardens or gardeners for them."

"Up!" said Ruby, "are we down below the world? Are we out of the world?"

Mavis smiled.

"I don't know," she said. "It may be up or it may be down. It doesn't matter. The princess says we may call it fairyland if we like. And fancy, Ruby, old Adam is the gardener here."

A shadow passed over Ruby's face.

"Don't be frightened, dear. He knew you were coming, and he's as kind as kind. We're to have supper at his cottage before we go home."

"Oh," said Ruby disappointed, "then we are to go home?"

"Oh yes," Mavis explained, "it wouldn't do for us to stay always here. But I *think* we may come back again sometimes. Adam has been often here, ever since he was a boy, he told me. And now he's going to stay always, till it's time for him to go somewhere else, he says. It was too cold and rough for him up by the sea now he is so old."

"And—about Winfried?" asked Ruby, growing very red.

Mavis laughed joyously.

"Winfried," she cried, "why, he was here already when I came; the boat went down, down with me, Ruby, when the great waves rolled over it and me. I *was* frightened, just for a minute, and then it was all right, and the princess and Winfried lifted me out."

"How many days ago was it?" asked Ruby.

Mavis shook her head.

"I don't know that either; perhaps it's not days at all here. I've never thought about it. But cousin Hortensia won't be frightened. The princess told me that. Winfried will take us home. He can't stay here either; he's got work to do somewhere, and he can only come back sometimes. There, Ruby —look—there he comes; do you see him coming up that little hill? He'll be here in a few minutes."

CHAPTER XI.

DOWN THE WELL.

RUBY shrank back a little.

"I don't want to see Winfried," she said, "after all we did. And, oh Mavis, I must be in such a mess — my clothes were all soaked in the sea."

"No, they weren't," said Mavis, laughing: "at least if they were they've come right again. Stand up, Ruby, and shake yourself, and look at yourself. There now, did you ever look neater or nicer in your life?"

Ruby stood up and looked at herself as Mavis advised her.

"Is this my own frock?" she said. "No, it can't be. See, Mavis, it's all beautifully embroidered with forget-me-nots! And what lovely blue ribbon my hair is tied with; and my hands are so white and clean — Mavis, did the princess dress me while I was asleep?"

Mavis nodded her head sagely.

"Something like it," she said.

"And oh," continued Ruby, "your frock is just the same, and your ribbons and all. *How* nice you look, Mavis! Is the princess here? I should so like her to see us."

"She's not here to-day," said Mavis. "She's away somewhere — I'm not sure," she added in a lower voice, "but that it's about Bertrand."

Ruby gave a sort of shiver.

"Oh Mavis!" she said, "he was so cruel and so heartless, and I was so miserable. I do hope the princess will make him go quite away."

"Or — if he was to be quite changed," said Mavis.

"No, no. I don't want him. I only want you, my darling little Mavis, and we shall be so happy — much, much happier than we have ever been. Kiss me, Mavis, and tell me you quite forgive me, and if ever I am naughty or horrid again, I hope the princess will punish me."

"She won't let you forget her anyway," said Mavis. "I think that is how she punishes."

Ruby looked rather puzzled; but before she could ask more they heard Winfried's whistle, and in a moment he appeared. His face was all one smile — all Ruby's fears and misgivings faded away before it.

"Grandfather is waiting for you," he said. "There are some cakes. Miss Ruby, that you will find even better than those others. For *everything* is better here, you see."

"How lovely it must all be," said Ruby, with a little sigh. "Aren't you sorry, Winfried, that you can't stay here altogether? Mavis says you have to go away to work."

"Of course," said Winfried cheerily. "It would never do, young as I am, not to work. And we shouldn't enjoy this half as much if we had it always — it's the rest and refreshment after common life that makes half the happiness. It's different for gran — he's done *his* part, none better, and now his work should be light. I'm thankful to know he's safe here. Now we had better go — down that little hill is the way to his cottage."

Children, you have perhaps never been in fairyland, nor, for that matter, have I been there either. But I have had glimpses of it a good many times in my life, and so I hope have you. And these glimpses, do you know, become more frequent and are less fleeting as one grows older. I, at least, find it so. Is not that something to look forward to? Though, after all, this sweet country to which our three little friends, thanks to the beautiful princess, had found their way, was scarcely the dream region which we think of as fairyland; it was better described by little Mavis's own name for the nameless garden — "Forget-me-not Land"; for once having entered there, no one can lose the remembrance of it, any more than once having looked into *her* eyes one can forget Princess Forget-me-not herself.

But it would be difficult to describe this magic land; I must leave a good deal of it to that kind of fancy which comes nearer truth than clumsy words. Though, as it is nice to be told all that *can* be told of the sweetest and most beautiful things, I will try to tell you a little of what Ruby and Mavis saw.

It might not have seemed such a lovely place to everybody, perhaps. Time had been even when Ruby herself might not have thought it so; for this garden-land was not a gorgeous place; it was just sweet and restful. As I told you, all the flowers were wild flowers; but that gives you no idea of what they looked like, for they were carefully tended and arranged, growing in great masses together in a way we never see, except sometimes in spring when the primroses almost hide the ground where they grow, or at mid-summer when a rich luxuriance of dog-roses and honeysuckle makes it seem as if they had been "planted on purpose," as children say. All along the grassy paths where Winfried led them, every step made the little girls exclaim in new admiration.

"Oh see, Ruby, there is a whole bank of 'ragged Robin.' I could not have believed it would look so beautiful; and there — look at those masses of 'sweet Cicely,' just like snowflakes. And in *our* fields it is such a poor frightened little weed of a flower you scarcely notice it," said Mavis.

"But it's lovely if you look into it closely," said

"Stop a moment," said the boy. "Stop and listen—hush—there now, do you hear them ringing?" p. 149

Winfried. "Some of the very tiniest flowers are really the most beautiful."

Then they came in sight of a stretch of hair-bells — white and blue — the kind that in some places are called "blue-bells."

"Stop a moment," said the boy. "Stop and listen — hush — there now, do you hear them ringing? That is a sound you can never hear in — anywhere but here."

They listened with all their ears, you may be sure. Yes, as they grew accustomed to the exceeding stillness, to the clear thin *fineness* of the air, they heard the softest, sweetest tinkle you can imagine; a perfect fairy bell-ringing, and the longer they listened the clearer it grew.

"Oh, how wonderful!" said Mavis.

And Ruby added, "I should think if we lived long enough in this country we should end by hearing the grass growing."

"Perhaps," said Winfried.

"But don't you miss the sea things?" Ruby went on. "You love them so, Winfried, and somehow you seem to belong to the sea."

"So I do," the boy replied. "The sea is my life. Coming here is only a rest and a holiday."

"I wonder," said Mavis, "I wonder if there is a garden country for the sea to match this for the land. A place where seaweeds and corals and all the loveliest sea things are taken care of, like the wild flowers here?"

"You may be sure there is," said the fisher-boy, smiling. "There is no saying what the princess won't have to show us, and where she won't take us now she has us in hand. Why, only to look into her eyes, you can see it—they seem to reach to everywhere; everywhere and everything beautiful seems in them."

"You have seen farther into them than we have," said Mavis thoughtfully. "But still I think I can understand what you mean."

"So can I, a *very* little," said Ruby. "But—they are rather frightening too, don't you think?"

"They must be at first," said Winfried.

But just then, a little way off, they caught sight of old Adam coming to meet them. His cottage was close by; they came upon it suddenly, for it stood half-hidden under the shelter of the hill they had been descending. Such a lovely cottage it was—so simple, yet so pretty; *quite* clean, with a cleanness you never see out of fairyland or places of that kind, with flowers of all kinds, forget-me-nots above all, clustering about it and peeping in at the windows.

Adam welcomed his little guests as kindly as if no unkind thought of him had ever entered Ruby's head; he made no difference between her and Mavis, and I think this caused Ruby to feel more sorry than anything could have done.

If they had been happy that afternoon in the cottage by the sea, you can fancy how happy they were in this wonderful new fairy home of the good old man's. There was no end to the things he had to show them and teach them, mostly, I think, about flowers; things they had never dreamt of, beauties of form and colour such as it would be impossible for me to describe. And each time they came to see him he promised to show and teach them still more. But at last Winfried said they must be going.

"I promised the princess," he said, for now he spoke of her quite openly to the children, "that I would take you home by the time the sun sets beside the castle, and it must be near that now."

"And how are we to go home?" asked Ruby.

"The boat is ready," Winfried answered.

"But where's the sea for it to sail on?" whispered Ruby to Mavis. She had not the courage to ask Winfried any more.

"Wait and see," said Mavis. "I don't know, but it is sure to be all right."

Then they bade Adam farewell, promising to come to visit him again whenever they should be allowed to do so — and rather wondering where Winfried was going to take them, they set off.

There was some reason for Ruby's question, for so far they had seen no water at all in Forget-me-not Land. Everything seemed fresh and fragrant, as if there was no dearth of moisture, but there was neither lake, nor pond, nor running brook. Winfried mounted the hill a little way, then turning sharply, they found themselves in a sort of small wooded ravine or glen. Steps led down the steep sides to the bottom, which was a perfect thicket of ferns, mostly of the deep green delicate kind, which loves darkness and water.

Winfried stooped and lifted, by a ring fixed into it, a heavy stone.

"You won't be frightened," he said. "This is the way. We have to go down the well. I'll go first; you'll find it quite easy."

It scarcely looked so, for it was very dark. Winfried stepped in — there was a ladder against the side — and soon disappeared, all but his head, then Mavis, and lastly, trembling a little it must be confessed, Ruby. As soon as they were all inside, the stone lid shut itself down; but instead, as one might have expected, of this leaving them in darkness, a clear almost bright light shone upwards as if a large lamp had been lighted at the foot of the well, and without difficulty the children made their way down the ladder.

"That's very nice," said Ruby. " I was so afraid we were going to be in the dark."

" Were you, dear ? " said a voice whose sweet tones were not strange to her. "No fear of that when I have to do with things. Jump, that's right; here you are, and you too, Mavis."

The princess was standing in the boat, for the " well " widened out at one side into a little stream large enough to row along.

"The brook takes us to the river, and the river to the sea; that is your way home," she said. "Winfried will row, and you two shall nestle up to me."

She put an arm round each, and in silence, save for the gentle drip of the oars, the little boat made its way. It was a still evening, not yet dark, though growing dusk, and though they were back in the winter world by now the children felt no cold — who could have felt cold with the princess's mantle round them? They grew sleepy, too sleepy to notice how, as she had said, the brook turned into the river, and the river led on to the sea, the familiar sea, not more than a mile or two from the cove below the castle.

And it was only when the boat grated a little on the pebbly shore that both Ruby and Mavis started up to find themselves alone with Winfried. The princess had left them.

"I will go up to the door with you," said the boy. "Miss Hortensia is expecting you. See, there she is standing under the archway with a lantern."

"My darlings," said their cousin. "So Winfried has brought you safe home."

"And I must hurry back," said the fisher-lad. And almost before they could thank him or say goodnight, he had disappeared again in the fast-gathering gloom.

It seemed to the children as Miss Hortensia kissed them that *years* had passed since they had seen her or their home.

"Haven't you been dreadfully lonely without us all this time, dear cousin?" said Mavis.

"No, dears, not particularly so. It is a little later than usual, but when Winfried ran back to tell me he would bring you safe home, he said it might be so."

"Was it only *this* afternoon we went?" said Ruby wonderingly.

Miss Hortensia looked at her anxiously.

"My dear, are you very tired? You seem half asleep."

"I am rather sleepy," said Ruby. "Please may we go to bed at once."

"Certainly. I will tell Ulrica to take your supper upstairs. I do hope you haven't caught cold. We must shut the door;" for they were standing all this time at the entrance under the archway. "Bertrand is behind you, I suppose?"

The little girls looked at each other.

"We have not seen him for ever so long," they replied.

"He would not stay with me," said Ruby.

"I thought perhaps we should find him here," said Mavis.

Miss Hortensia looked more annoyed than anxious.

"I suppose he will find his way back before long," she said. "Bad pennies always turn up. But he is a most troublesome boy. I wish I had asked Winfried what to do—"

"I don't think he could have done anything," said Mavis. "But — I'm sure Bertrand is safe. What's the matter, Ulrica?"

For at that moment — they were on their way upstairs by this time — the young maid-servant came flying to meet them, her face pale, her eyes gleaming with fear.

"Oh," she cried, "I am glad the young ladies are safe back. Martin has seen the blue light in the west turret; he was coming from the village a few minutes ago, and something made him look up. It is many and many a year since it has been seen, not since the young ladies were babies, and it always —"

"Stop, Ulrica," said Miss Hortensia sharply. "It is very wrong of you to come startling us in that wild way, and the young ladies so tired as you see. Call Bertha and Joseph. You take the children to their room, and see that they are warm and comfortable. I will myself go up to the west turret with the others and put a stop to these idle tales."

But Ruby and Mavis pressed forward. A strange thought had struck them both.

"Oh cousin, let us go too," they said. "We are not a bit frightened."

So when old Joseph and Bertha had joined them, the whole party set off for the turret.

As they got near to the top of the stair, a slight sound made them all start.

"Hush!" said Miss Hortensia. They stood in

perfect silence. It came again — a murmur of faint sobs and weeping. Ulrica grew whiter and whiter. "I told you so," she began. but no one listened. They all pressed on, Miss Hortensia the first.

When she opened the door it was, except for the lamp she held in her hand, upon total darkness. But in one corner was heard a sort of convulsive breathing. and then a voice.

"Who's there? Who's there? Oh the pain, the cruel pain!"

And there — lying on the same little couch-bed on which years and years ago Miss Hortensia had slept and dreamt of the lovely fairy lady — was Bertrand — weeping and moaning, utterly broken down.

But he turned away sullenly from Miss Hortensia when she leant over him in concern and pity: he would not look at Ruby either, and it was not till after some moments had passed that they at last heard him whisper.

"Mavis, I want to speak to Mavis. Go away everybody. I only want Mavis."

They all looked at each other in mute astonishment. They thought he was wandering in his mind. But no, he kept to the same idea.

"Mavis," he repeated. "come here and give me your hand. I can't see you. Oh the pain, the pain!"

Then Mavis came forward, and the others drew back in a group to the door.

"Try and find out what it is: surely it is not another naughty trick that he is playing," said Miss Hortensia anxiously.

"No, no. I am sure it isn't. Don't be afraid, dear cousin," said the little girl.

CHAPTER XII.

> "The world that only thy spirit knows
> Is the fairest world of the three."
>
> THREE WORLDS.

"MAVIS," whispered Bertrand, when he was sure the others were out of earshot, "you can understand; they would think I was mad. Listen — stoop down — it is *she*. You know who I mean. She made me see her, and oh, the pain is too awful. It isn't only in my eyes, it goes down into my heart somehow. What shall I do? Can't you make her come to take it away? I've been crying and crying to her, but she won't."

"Perhaps it is that you *must* bear it," said Mavis. "Think that way, and see if that makes it any better."

The boy gasped, but did not speak. After a moment or two he went on again.

"I was in the caves behind the cottage. I ran in to get out of the storm, and because I didn't want to go looking for you. I thought you were drowned, and I didn't want to see your white face," he shivered. "And I was peeping about in one of the caves when I fell; I don't know how or where. I fell down, down, ever so far. I thought I was never going to stop, and then my breath went away, and I didn't know anything till I found myself in another cave, all knocked about and bruised. I'm aching now all over, but I don't mind that. And then, Mavis, *she* came and looked at me."

"You saw her?" said Mavis.

"Yes—oh Mavis, she made my eyes go up to hers. And oh, the pain! She didn't say anything except just 'Bertrand.' But I knew all she meant, better than by any speaking. And she was kind; she lifted me and carried me up here. And she put something on my leg; that was where I was most hurt, I think. Then she sat by me here, and she put it all into my mind, all the naughty things I'd ever done. Mavis, I didn't know, I *really* didn't, how bad I was. It came out of her eyes somehow, though I dared not look again; and when she went away, even though I *think* she kissed me, the pain got worse and worse. Oh Mavis, will it ever go? Will my eyes ever feel the same again?"

"No," said Mavis, "I don't think they'll ever feel the *same*, for they'll feel much, much better than they used to. The pain will go, though it may come back sometimes, to *remind* you."

"I shan't need reminding," said the boy. "I can't ever forget. I'm sure of that. I wish I could!"

"No, Bertrand, I don't think you do wish that."

He gave an impatient wriggle, but without speaking.

"Oh the pain," he cried again in a moment or two, "and it did seem a little better."

Miss Hortensia came forward.

"Mavis, my dear, what is it? Where is he hurt? And why did you hide yourself up here, Bertrand, instead of coming to me?"

Bertrand would not answer. He turned his face away again.

"He's had a fall, cousin Hortensia," said Mavis. "But I don't think it's very bad, he says he's only bruised and sore. Bertrand, do you think you can manage to get down to your own room?"

"If you'll come at one side and Joseph at the other, I'll try," said the boy, with unusual graciousness. "And when I'm in bed, will you stay beside me, Mavis? I think the pain isn't so bad when you're there," he whispered, so that no one else could hear.

Miss Hortensia was quick-witted.

"I will order a fire to be lighted in Bertrand's room," she said; "and if you like, Mavis, you may have your supper there beside him."

She hurried away, calling Ruby to go with her. It was a sign of a very different state of things with Ruby that she showed, and felt, no jealousy at Bertrand's preference for her sister.

"Poor Bertrand," she said to herself softly, "perhaps I made him naughtier than he would have been."

The boy was more hurt than he would allow, but he put great constraint on himself, and limped downstairs with scarcely a groan.

"It's nothing compared to the other pain." he murmured. And when he was at last safely deposited in his little bed, he looked so white and pitiful that for the first time Mavis stooped down and gave him a loving kiss. Bertrand started.

" What is it?" said Mavis.

" I don't know," he replied. " When you kissed me, the pain got worse for a moment; it gave a great stab, but now it seems better. If you'll kiss me again, Mavis, the last thing when you say goodnight. perhaps I'll be able to go to sleep."

She stayed beside him all the rest of the evening. He scarcely spoke, only groaning a little from time to time. When Miss Hortensia came in to send Mavis to bed, she began for the first time to feel really uneasy about the boy.

" Mavis." she said, not meaning Bertrand to hear, " if he isn't better to-morrow morning. we must send for the doctor."

" Perhaps," said the little girl. " he could do something to take away the aching — poor Bertrand is aching all over from his fall."

" I don't mind that," said the boy suddenly. " It isn't that, you know it isn't. Mavis, and I won't have the doctor."

Ruby, who had stolen in behind her cousin, crept up to Mavis.

"Do you think," she whispered, "do you think, Mavis, that he has seen *her*, and that that's it?"

Mavis did not answer.

"Bertrand," she said, "we are going to bed now; do you mind being left alone for the night?"

"No," he said, "I'd rather, unless it was you, and you can't stay. You'd be too tired. Listen," and he drew her down to him, "do you think perhaps she'll come again and take away the pain? For I *am* sorry now — I am sorry — and I didn't know how bad I was."

"Poor Bertrand," whispered Mavis pityingly. "Perhaps she will come. Anyway, if you are patient and try to think the pain has to be, I think it will get better, even if it doesn't go away altogether."

And again she kissed him.

"Mavis," said Ruby, as the two little sisters were lying side by side in their white curtained beds, "cousin Hortensia may not know it, and nobody may know it, but *I* know it, and it is that years have passed since we went to bed here last night."

"Yes," said Mavis. "I think so too. There are some things that you can't count time for, which are really far more than any time."

"All my hating of Bertrand has gone away now," continued Ruby. "Only I don't want him to stay here, because the naughty in him and the naughty in me might get together again like it did before."

"Why don't you think of the good in him and the good in you joining to make you both better; and the good in me too? I suppose it isn't conceited to think there is a little good in oneself, at least there's trying to be and wanting to be," said Mavis, with a little sigh. "But you're so much quicker and cleverer than I am, Ruby, I wish you would think about helping me and not about being naughty. And, oh Ruby, isn't it lovely to think that we may go sometimes to Forget-me-not Land?"

"Let's go to sleep now as quick as we can and dream of it," said Ruby.

Bertrand looked still very white and ill the next day. He was very quiet and subdued, and even gave in to Miss Hortensia's decision that the doctor must be sent for. The doctor came "and shook his head." The boy was not in a satisfactory condition, — which they knew already as it happened, otherwise the doctor would not have been sent for, — he had been shaken by the fall, and it was possible that his back had been injured. There was not much comfort in all this, certainly, but it decided one thing, that he was to stay where he was for the present, not to attempt to get up or to move about. And, strange to say, this too Bertrand accepted uncomplainingly.

He said no word to the doctor of the strange pain he had confided about to Mavis; and though his eyes seemed sad and wearied, they had a new look in them which had never been there before. Even Miss Hortensia was moved by it, though hitherto, and rightly. she had been inclined to treat Bertrand's troubles as well deserved.

"Is there anything we can do for you, my poor boy?" she said kindly.

"No, thank you," he replied; "except to let Mavis come to stay beside me sometimes — and —" he hesitated, "if the fisher-boy, Winfried, comes to the castle, I'd like to see him."

"Certainly," Miss Hortensia answered. "But I doubt if he will come any more. I hear in the village that his grandfather has gone away, quite away, to a milder part of the country. I can't understand it, it seems so sudden."

But Winfried did come, that very afternoon. His new home was not so very far away, he told Miss Hortensia with a smile. "Gran's home, that is to say," he went on. "But I myself am going to have a different kind of home now. I'm going to sea; I've always wished it, and gran has wished it for me."

"But won't he miss you terribly?" asked the lady.

"I'll often be with him, and he's well cared for where he is," said the boy.

And then Mavis took him up to see Bertrand, with whom she left him alone for some time.

There was a brighter look in the boy's face when she went back to him.

"Winfried has promised to come again before he goes quite away," he said. "Did you know, Mavis, that he is going ever so far away? He is going to be a sailor, a real sailor, not a fisherman. He says he has always wanted it, but he couldn't leave his grandfather alone here where the village people were not—" Bertrand stopped suddenly, as it struck him that it was not the ignorant village people only who had been unkind to good old Adam. Mavis understood but said nothing. And after a bit Bertrand went on again.

"Mavis," he said, "I've seen her again. Either I saw her or I dreamt of her. I don't much mind which it was, for it's all come true. She said I must try to bear it, like what you said. Mavis; and it has got better. But she said it would come back again, and that I'd get to want it to come back — at least, unless I wanted to forget her, and I don't want to do that. I don't think I *could*, even if I tried. And she kissed me — my eyes, Mavis: so you see I couldn't forget her now."

"You never could, I'm sure," said Mavis; "that's what she is; it's her name."

Bertrand threw himself back with a sigh.

"I can't feel like you," he said. "I've never thought about being good, and sometimes I think I won't try. Oh Mavis!"

"Was it the pain again?" said the little girl sympathisingly, though in her heart she felt inclined to smile a very little.

"Yes," said Bertrand dolefully, "I'm afraid it will take an awfully long time before I begin to get the least bit good," and he sighed again still more deeply.

Just then Ruby put her head in at the door. She and Bertrand were not yet quite at ease with each other, but she came up to his bedside very gently and said she hoped he was better, to which he replied meekly enough, though rather stiffly.

"Mavis," said Ruby eagerly, pleased to find something to talk about, "have you heard about Winfried? about his going to be a real sailor?"

"Yes," said Mavis. "Bertrand was talking about it."

Bertrand sat up and his eyes sparkled.

"I didn't mean to tell you," he said, "but I think I must. Do you know, I believe I shall be a sailor too? Papa has always wanted it since I was quite little, and I shall soon be old enough to begin. But I thought I wouldn't like it till I came here and saw the sea; and now Winfried's talking has made it come into my mind, just the way papa said it did into his when he was a boy."

Ruby glanced at him admiringly.

"How brave you are. Bertrand!" she said, which was a very foolish speech.

"No," he said with a touch of his old roughness, "I'm not. It isn't that at all. Mavis, would you be glad for me to be a sailor?"

"If you found it the best thing for you I'd be glad," said Mavis. "Sailors must see wonderful and beautiful things," she went on thoughtfully.

"Perhaps you and Winfried might be sailors together some time," said Ruby. "That would be nice."

"Yes," said Bertrand. "When I got to be captain or something like that, I'll look him up, and —" but he stopped abruptly. There had been a touch of arrogance in his tone.

Just then Ruby ran off. Mavis was going too, but Bertrand stopped her.

"Mavis," he said, "Winfried knows all about *her*. He calls her his princess."

"I know," said Mavis.

"And," Bertrand went on, "he says he knows she'll never be far away if he wants her. Even *ever* so far away, over at the other side of the world, out at sea with no land for weeks and months; he says it would be just the same, or even better. The loneliness makes it easier to see her sometimes, he says. I can fancy that," he went on dreamily, "her eyes are a little like the sea, don't you think, Mavis?"

"Like the sea when it is *quite* good, quite at peace, loving and gentle," she replied. "But still, if you had lived beside the sea as long as we have, Bertrand, you'd understand that there's never a sure feeling about it, you never know what it won't be doing next; and the princess, you know, makes you feel surer than sure; that's the best of her."

"Yes," said Bertrand, "the sea's like Ruby and me. Now just at this time I want more than anything to be good, and never to be selfish or cruel, or — or boasting, or mischievous. But when I get about again with Ruby — even though she's very good now, and she never was anything like as bad as me — I don't feel sure but what we might do each other harm and forget about being good and all that; do you see?"

"I think it's a very good thing that you do *not* feel sure," said Mavis. But she was struck by his saying just what Ruby herself had said, and it made her a little anxious.

The children's new resolutions, however, were not put to the test in the way they expected. Bertrand quickly got well again and was able to run about in his usual way. But very soon after this his uncle, the father of Ruby and Mavis, came unexpectedly for one of his short visits to the castle, to his little daughters' great delight. And when he left he took Bertrand away with him. There was more than one reason for the boy's visit coming to an end so much sooner than had been intended. Miss Hortensia may have had something to do with it, for though she had grown to like Bertrand much better during his illness, and no one could have been more delighted than she at the improvement in him, it was not to be wondered at if she trembled at continuing to have the charge of him. Then, too, Bertrand confided to his uncle his wish to be a sailor, in which he never again wavered.

Ruby and Mavis felt sad when the travellers had left them. Their father's "good-byes" were the only alloy to the pleasure of his visits. And this time there was Bertrand to say good-bye to also!

"Who would have thought," said Mavis, "that we should ever be sorry to see him go? But I am glad to feel sorry."

"Yes," said Miss Hortensia, "much better for him to go while his present mood lasts, and we are able to regret him. And maybe he will come to pay us a visit again some time or other."

"I hope he will," said Mavis. "I don't think he will *ever* again be like what he was, cousin."

"Mavis," said Ruby, when they were alone, "when Bertrand does come to see us again, we must plan all to go to Forget-me-not Land together. It would be so nice, all four of us. Winfried will come to see us again soon; he said he would whenever he comes to his grandfather; let us ask him. I am sure the princess wouldn't mind now Bertrand is so different."

"I am sure she wouldn't," said Mavis, smiling.

"And who knows," Ruby went on, "what lovely new things and places we shan't see when we go there again. Winfried says there's no end to

them, and that every time we go we'll find more to
see."

"Perhaps it's because we learn to see better and
better," said Mavis.

And I think she was right.

THE END.

www.ingramcontent.com/pod-product-compliance
Lightning Source LLC
Chambersburg PA
CBHW021717110726
47902CB00005B/1230